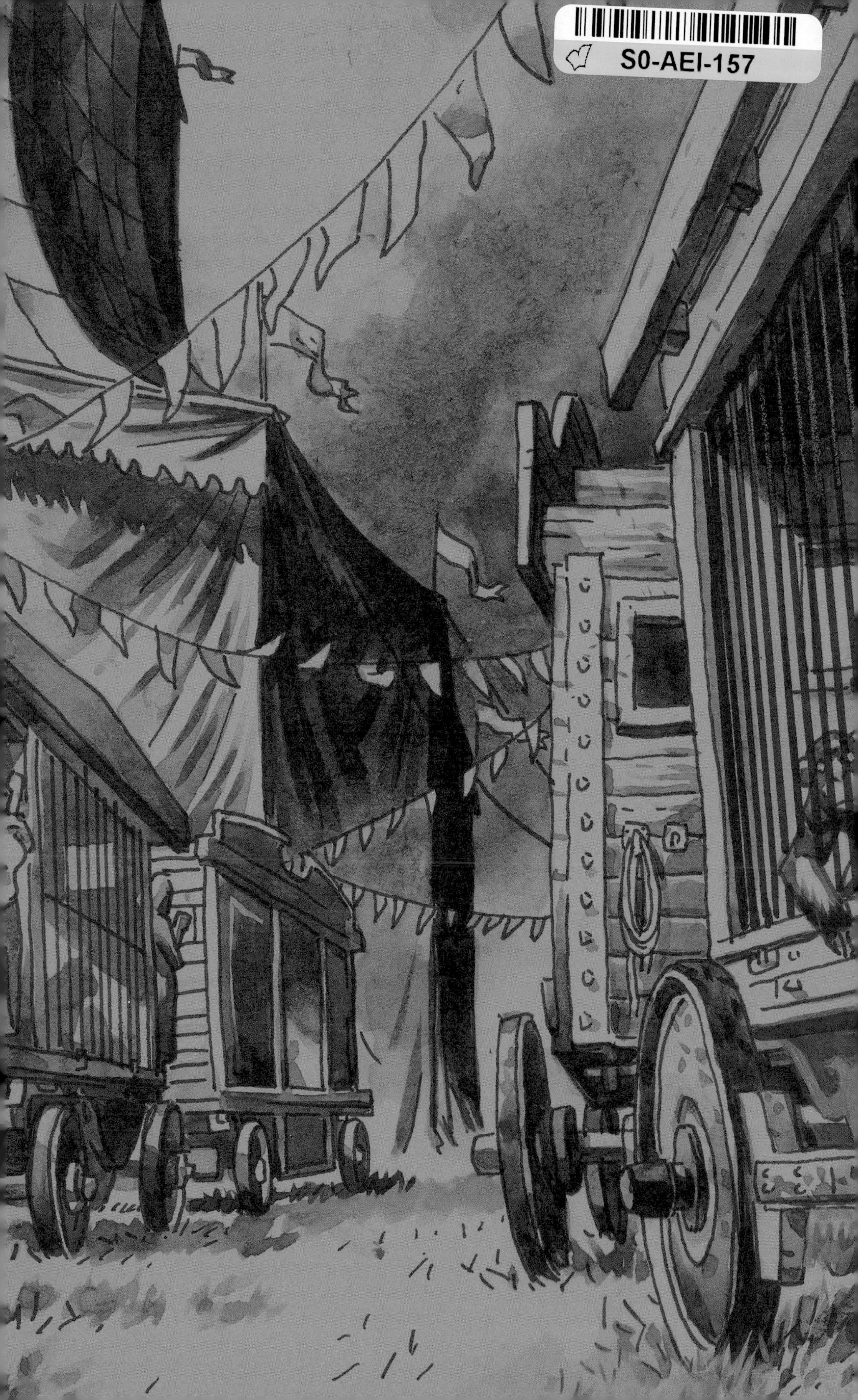

HELLBOY™

THE MIDNIGHT CIRCUS

ZINC

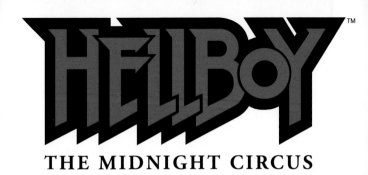

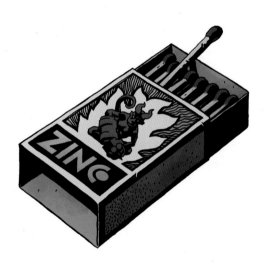

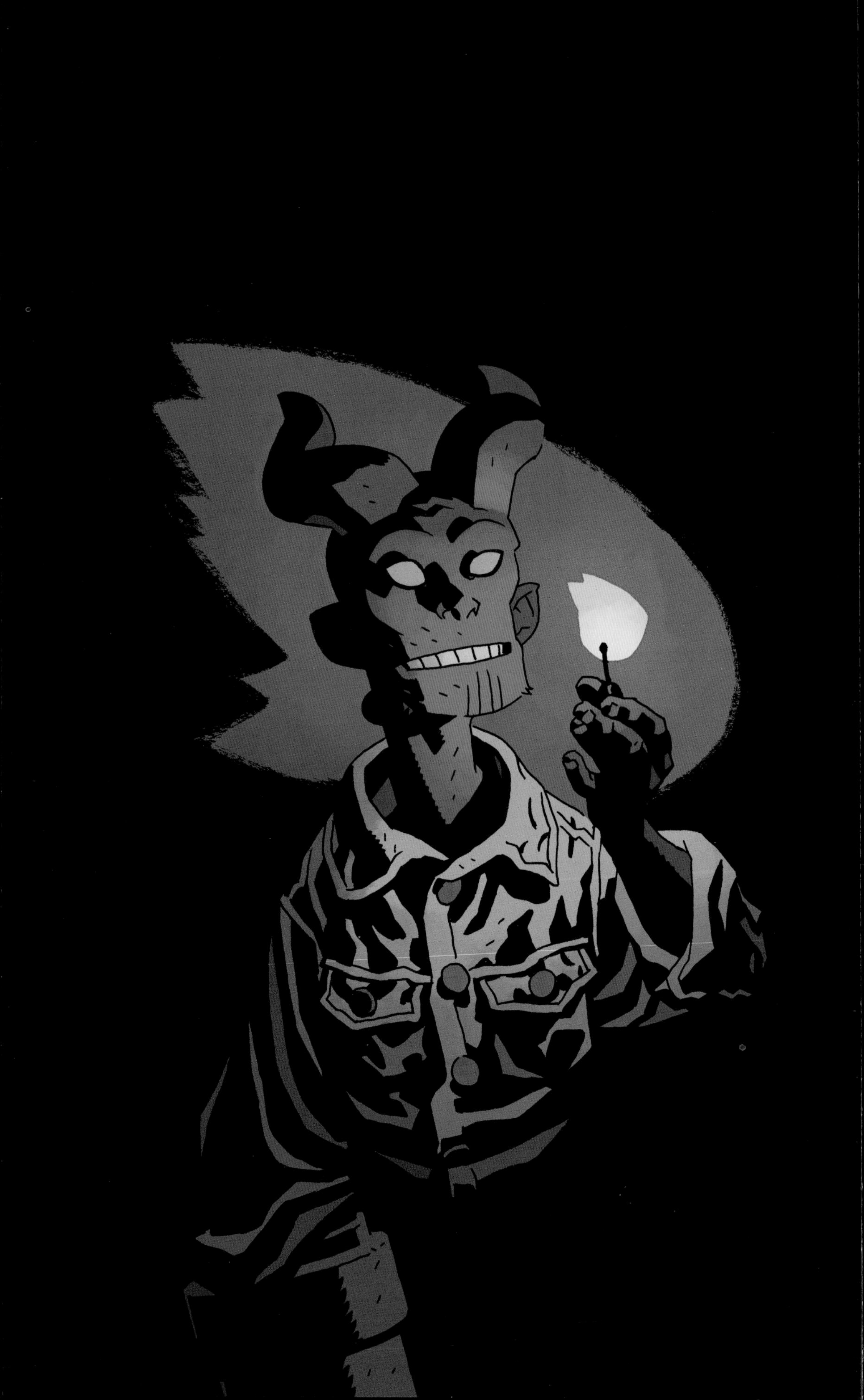

HELLBOY ™

THE MIDNIGHT CIRCUS

Story by
MIKE MIGNOLA

Art by
DUNCAN FEGREDO

Colored by
DAVE STEWART

Lettered by
CLEM ROBINS

✠

Cover art by
MIKE MIGNOLA & DAVE STEWART

Editor
SCOTT ALLIE

Associate Editor
DANIEL CHABON

Hellboy logo designed by
KEVIN NOWLAN

Collection designed by
MIKE MIGNOLA & CARY GRAZZINI

Publisher
MIKE RICHARDSON

DARK HORSE BOOKS

Mike Richardson ✠ *President and Publisher*

Neil Hankerson ✠ *Executive Vice President*

Tom Weddle ✠ *Chief Financial Officer*

Randy Stradley ✠ *Vice President of Publishing*

Michael Martens ✠ *Vice President of Book Trade Sales*

Anita Nelson ✠ *Vice President of Business Affairs*

Scott Allie ✠ *Editor in Chief*

Matt Parkinson ✠ *Vice President of Marketing*

David Scroggy ✠ *Vice President of Product Development*

Dale LaFountain ✠ *Vice President of Information Technology*

Darlene Vogel ✠ *Senior Director of Print, Design, and Production*

Ken Lizzi ✠ *General Counsel*

Davey Estrada ✠ *Editorial Director*

Chris Warner ✠ *Senior Books Editor*

Diana Schutz ✠ *Executive Editor*

Cary Grazzini ✠ *Director of Print and Development*

Lia Ribacchi ✠ *Art Director*

Cara Niece ✠ *Director of Scheduling*

Tim Wiesch ✠ *Director of International Licensing*

Mark Bernardi ✠ *Director of Digital Publishing*

Published by
Dark Horse Books
A division of Dark Horse Comics, Inc.
10956 SE Main Street
Milwaukie, OR 97222

International Licensing: (503) 905-2377

First edition
October 2013
ISBN 978-1-61655-238-1

1 3 5 7 9 10 8 6 4 2

Printed in China

For Carlo Collodi, who taught me everything I know about what a puppet should be. And for Ray Bradbury, who confirmed my worst fears about the circus.

MIKE MIGNOLA

For my mum—she always knew better, yet still didn't dissuade me from running away to join the circus.

DUNCAN FEGREDO

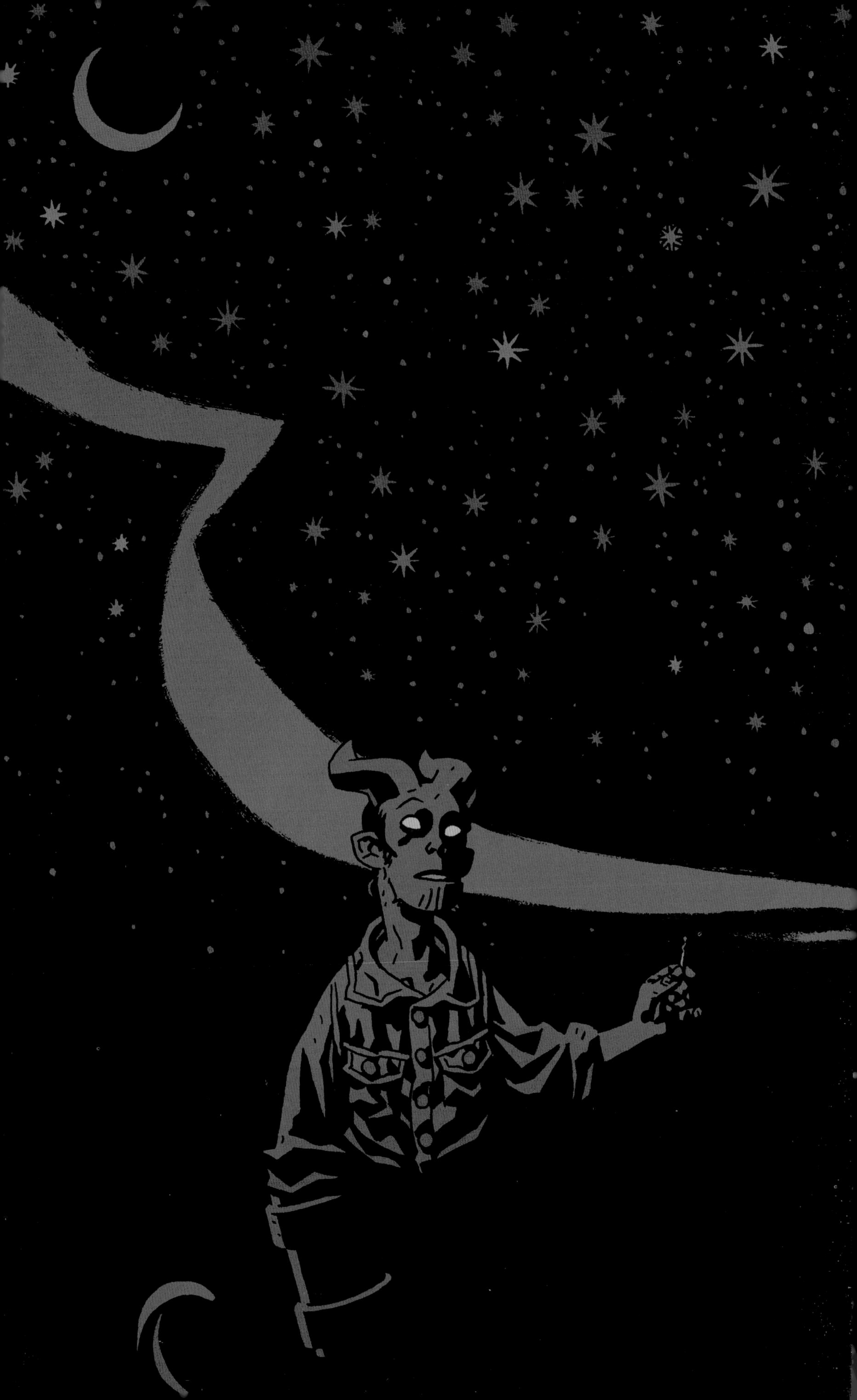

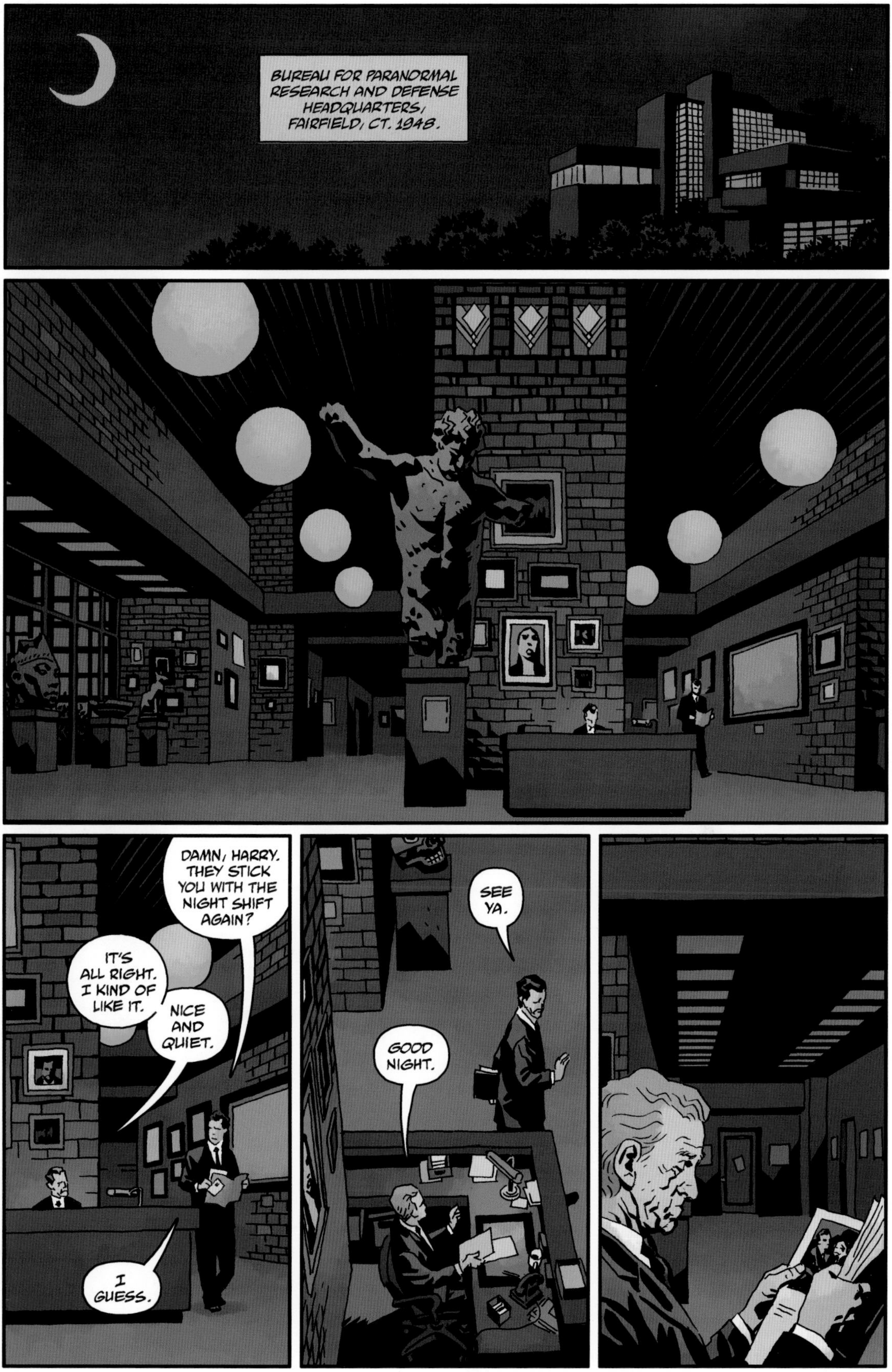
BUREAU FOR PARANORMAL RESEARCH AND DEFENSE HEADQUARTERS, FAIRFIELD, CT. 1948.
DAMN, HARRY. THEY STICK YOU WITH THE NIGHT SHIFT AGAIN?
IT'S ALL RIGHT. I KIND OF LIKE IT.
NICE AND QUIET.
I GUESS.
SEE YA.
GOOD NIGHT.

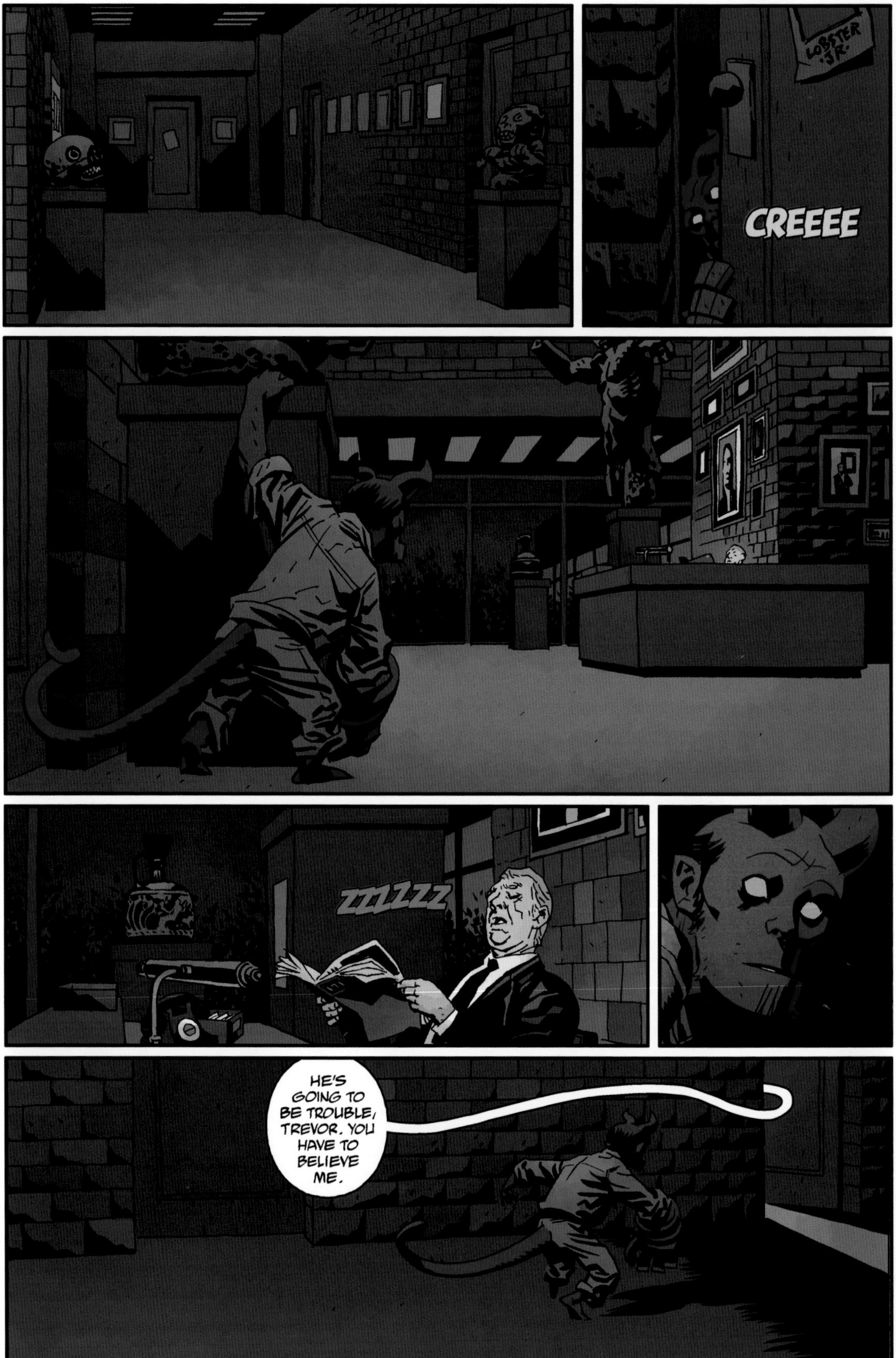
LOBSTER JR.
CREEEE
ZZZZZZ
HE'S GOING TO BE TROUBLE, TREVOR. YOU HAVE TO BELIEVE ME.

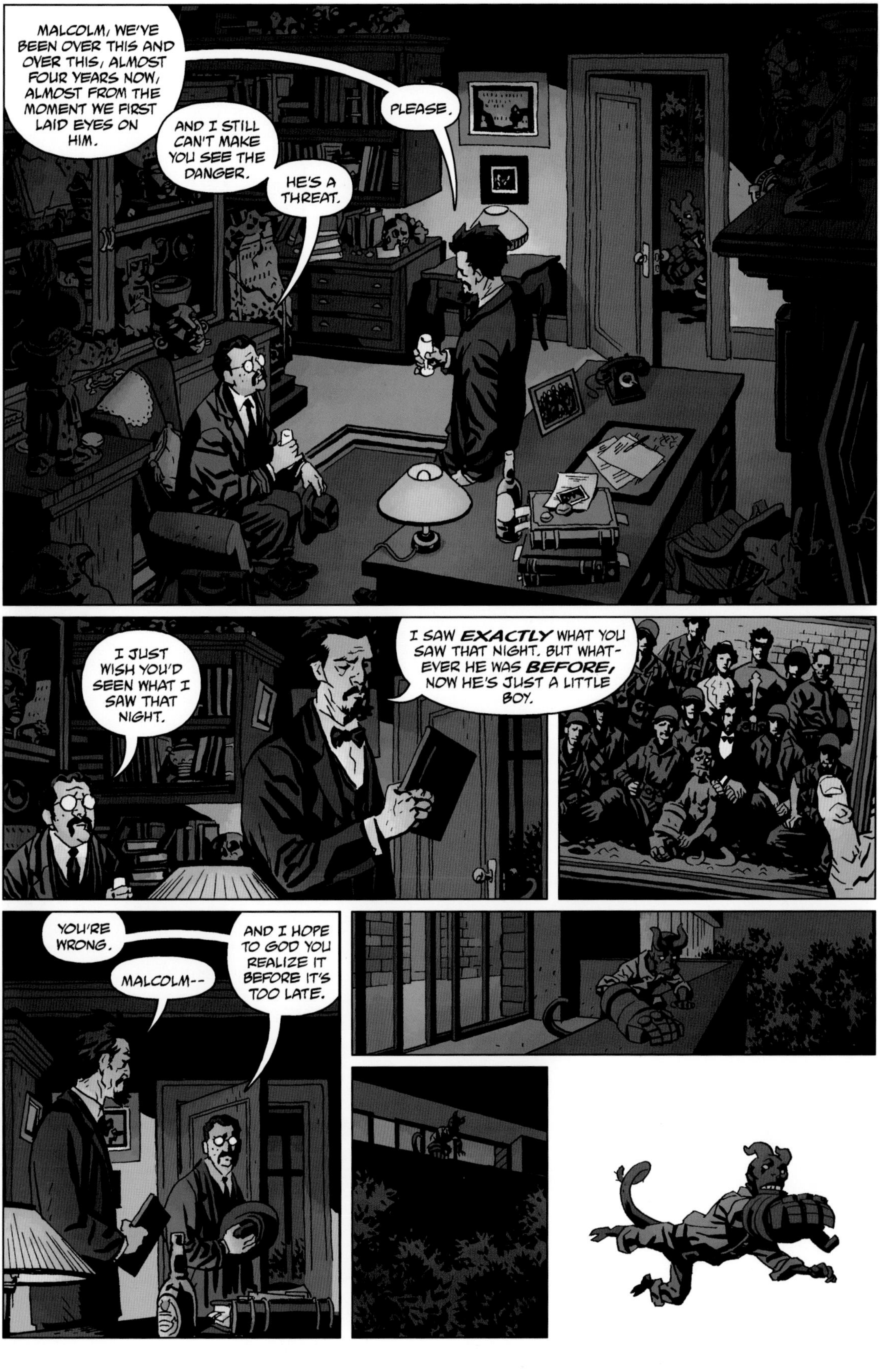
MALCOLM, WE'VE BEEN OVER THIS AND OVER THIS, ALMOST FOUR YEARS NOW, ALMOST FROM THE MOMENT WE FIRST LAID EYES ON HIM.
PLEASE.
AND I STILL CAN'T MAKE YOU SEE THE DANGER.
HE'S A THREAT.
I JUST WISH YOU'D SEEN WHAT I SAW THAT NIGHT.
I SAW EXACTLY WHAT YOU SAW THAT NIGHT. BUT WHATEVER HE WAS BEFORE, NOW HE'S JUST A LITTLE BOY.
YOU'RE WRONG.
MALCOLM--
AND I HOPE TO GOD YOU REALIZE IT BEFORE IT'S TOO LATE.

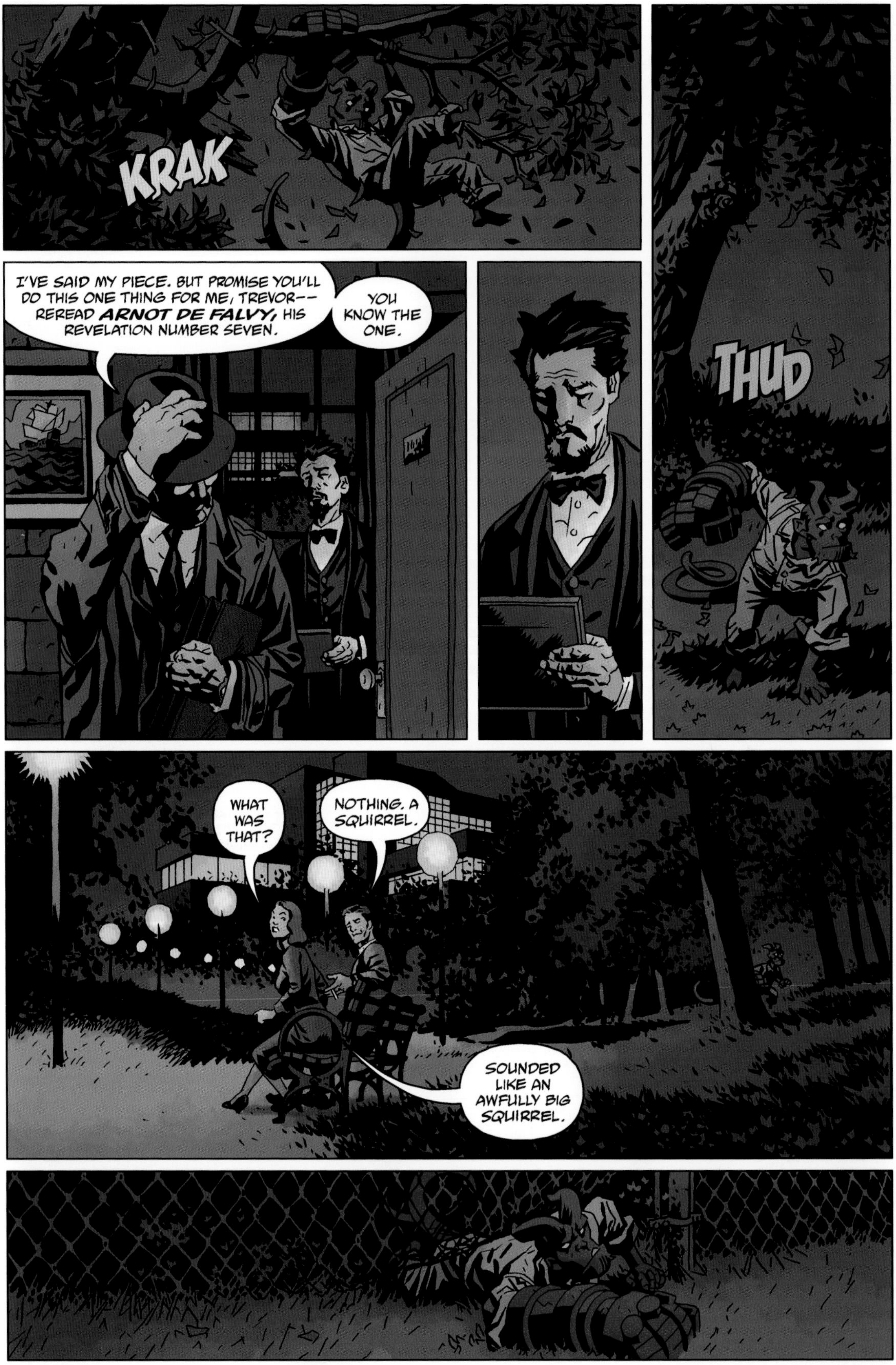
KRAK
I'VE SAID MY PIECE. BUT PROMISE YOU'LL DO THIS ONE THING FOR ME, TREVOR-- REREAD ARNOT DE FALVY, HIS REVELATION NUMBER SEVEN.
YOU KNOW THE ONE.
THUD
WHAT WAS THAT?
NOTHING. A SQUIRREL.
SOUNDED LIKE AN AWFULLY BIG SQUIRREL.

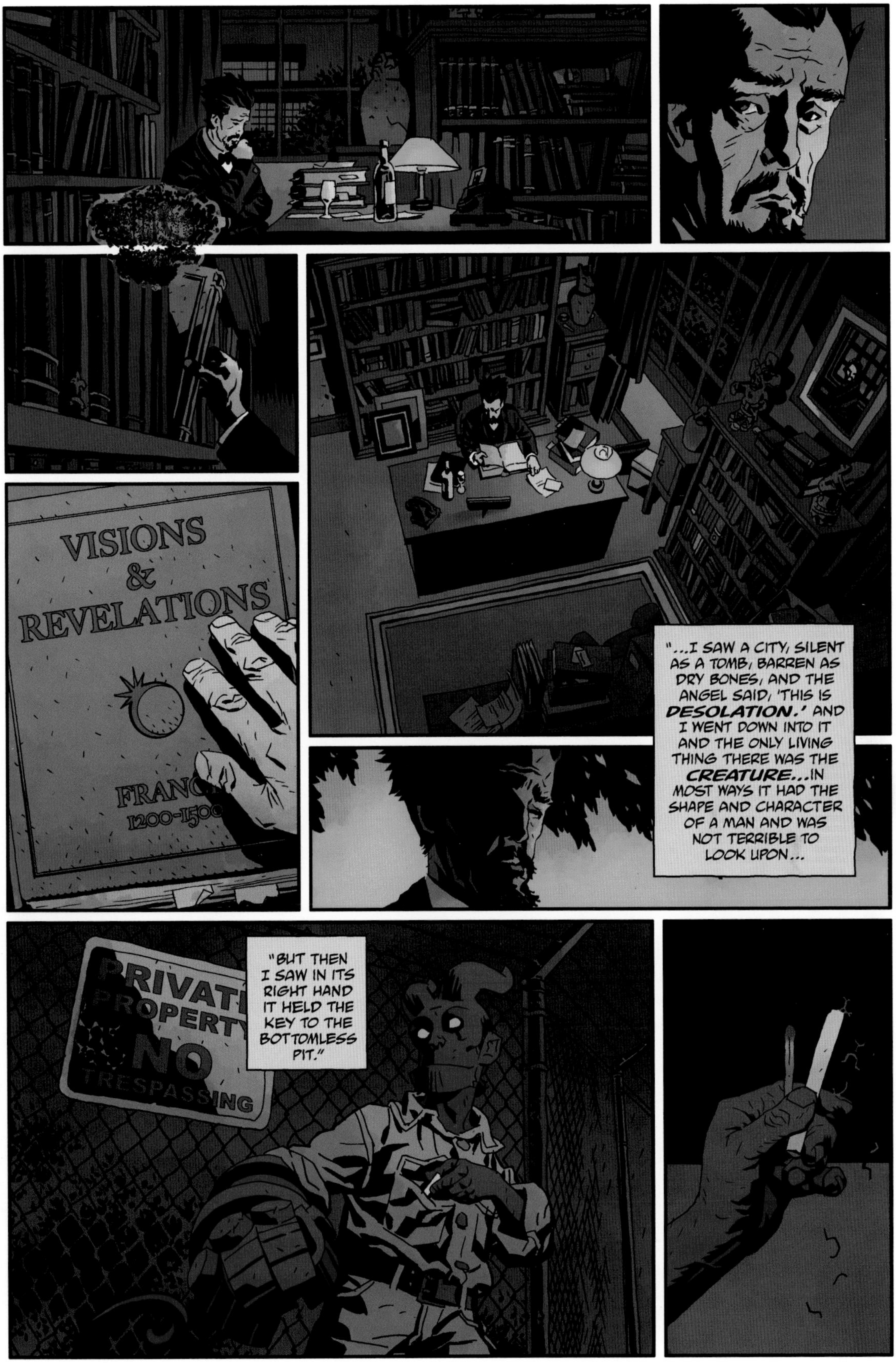
VISIONS & REVELATIONS
FRANC
1200-1500
"...I SAW A CITY, SILENT AS A TOMB, BARREN AS DRY BONES, AND THE ANGEL SAID, 'THIS IS DESOLATION.' AND I WENT DOWN INTO IT AND THE ONLY LIVING THING THERE WAS THE CREATURE...IN MOST WAYS IT HAD THE SHAPE AND CHARACTER OF A MAN AND WAS NOT TERRIBLE TO LOOK UPON...
TRESPASSING
"BUT THEN I SAW IN ITS RIGHT HAND IT HELD THE KEY TO THE BOTTOMLESS PIT."

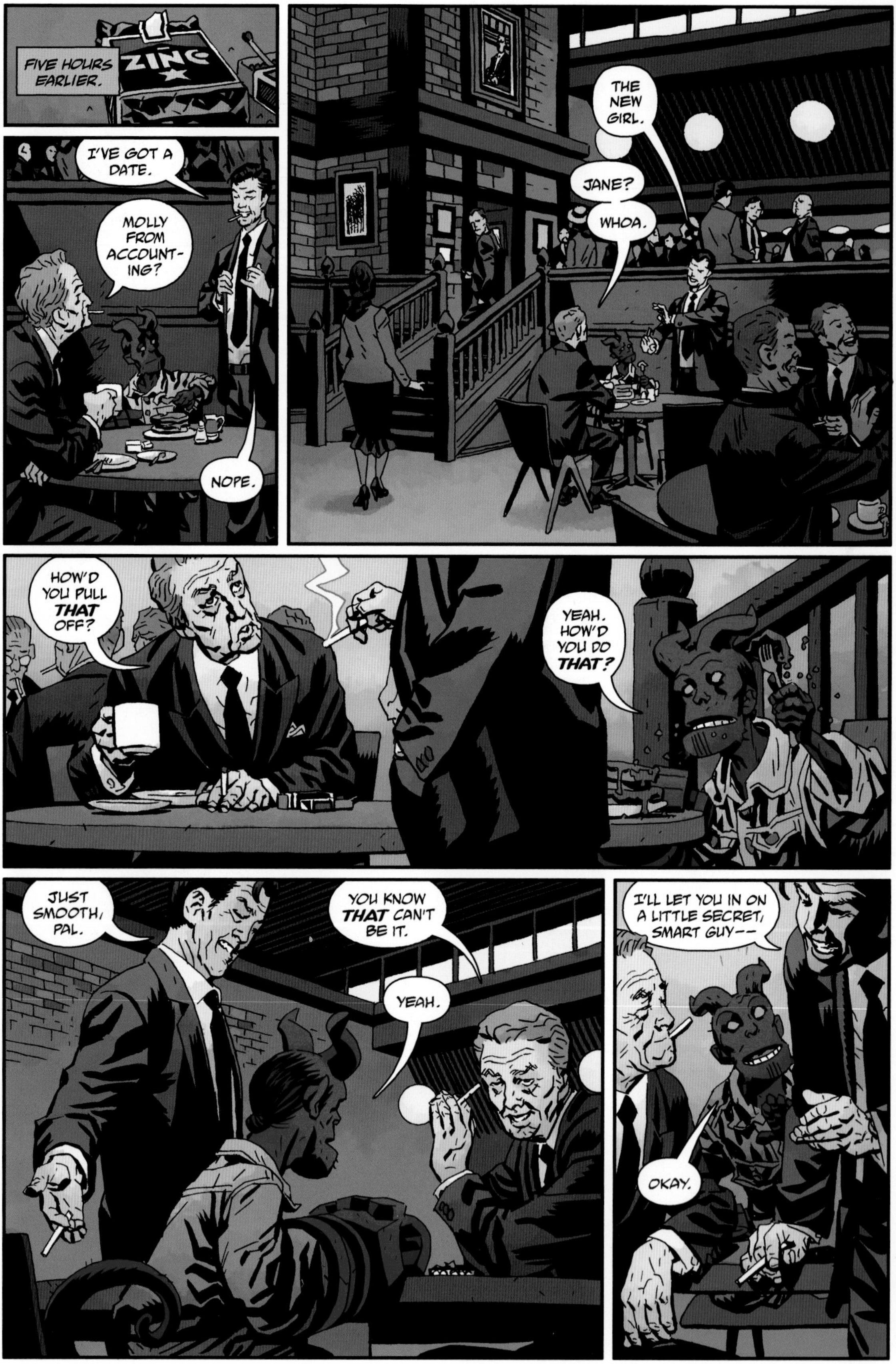
FIVE HOURS EARLIER.
ZINC
I'VE GOT A DATE.
MOLLY FROM ACCOUNTING?
NOPE.
THE NEW GIRL.
JANE?
WHOA.
HOW'D YOU PULL *THAT* OFF?
YEAH. HOW'D YOU DO *THAT?*
JUST SMOOTH, PAL.
YOU KNOW *THAT* CAN'T BE IT.
YEAH.
I'LL LET YOU IN ON A LITTLE SECRET, SMART GUY--
OKAY.

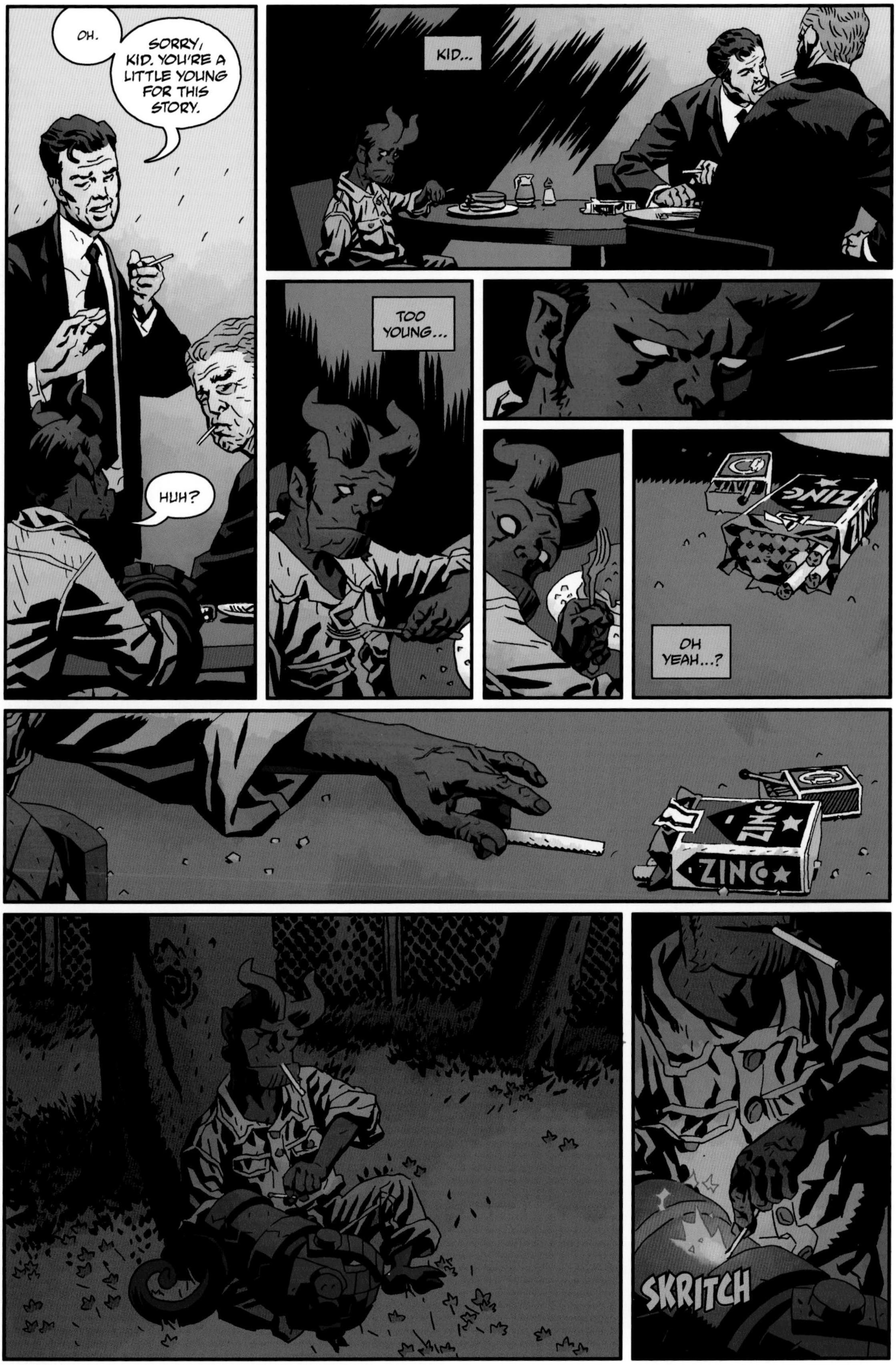
OH.
SORRY, KID. YOU'RE A LITTLE YOUNG FOR THIS STORY.
HUH?
KID...
TOO YOUNG...
OH YEAH...?
ZINC
ZINC
ZINC
SKRITCH

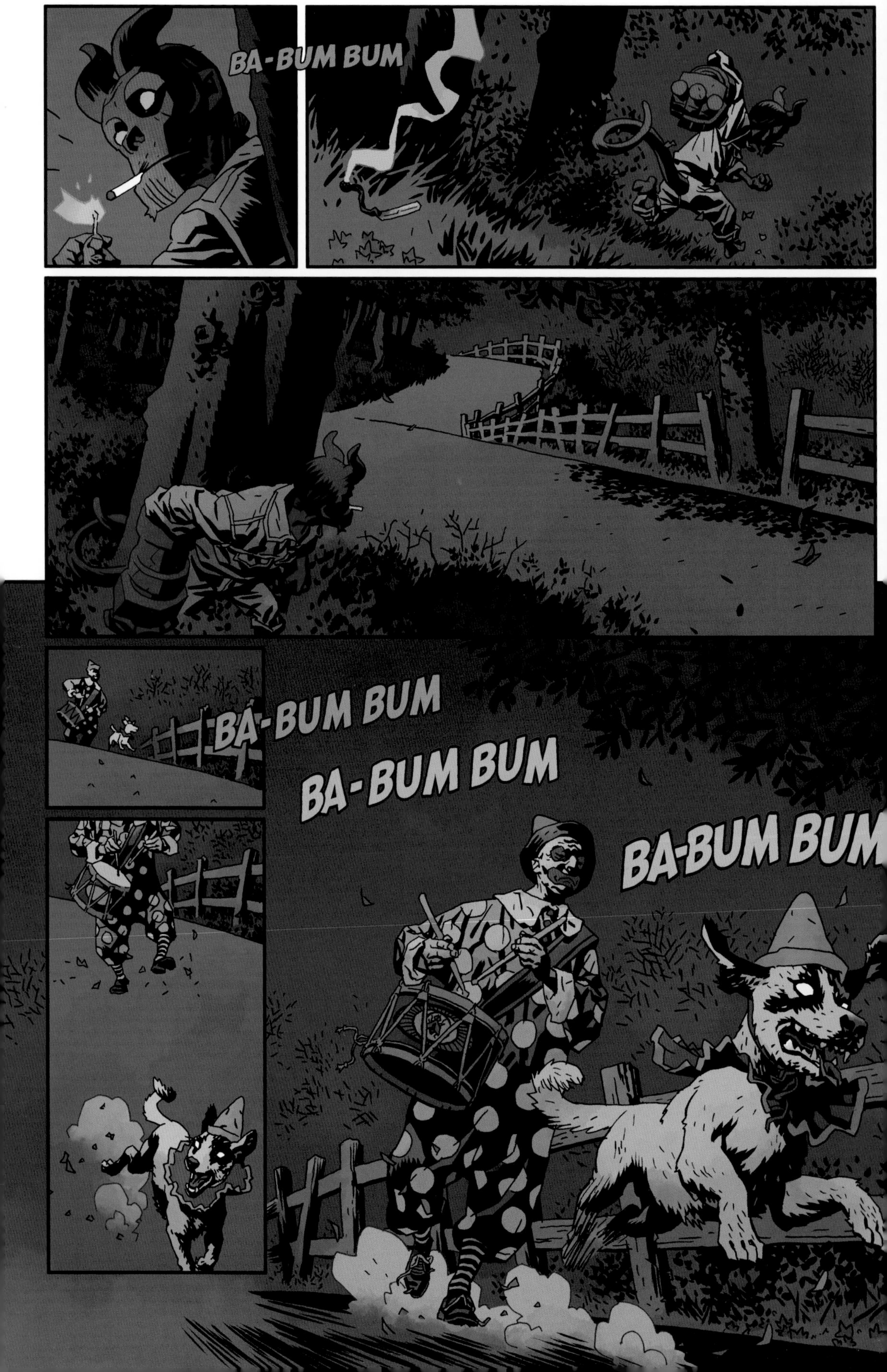
BA-BUM BUM
BA-BUM BUM
BA-BUM BUM
BA-BUM BUM

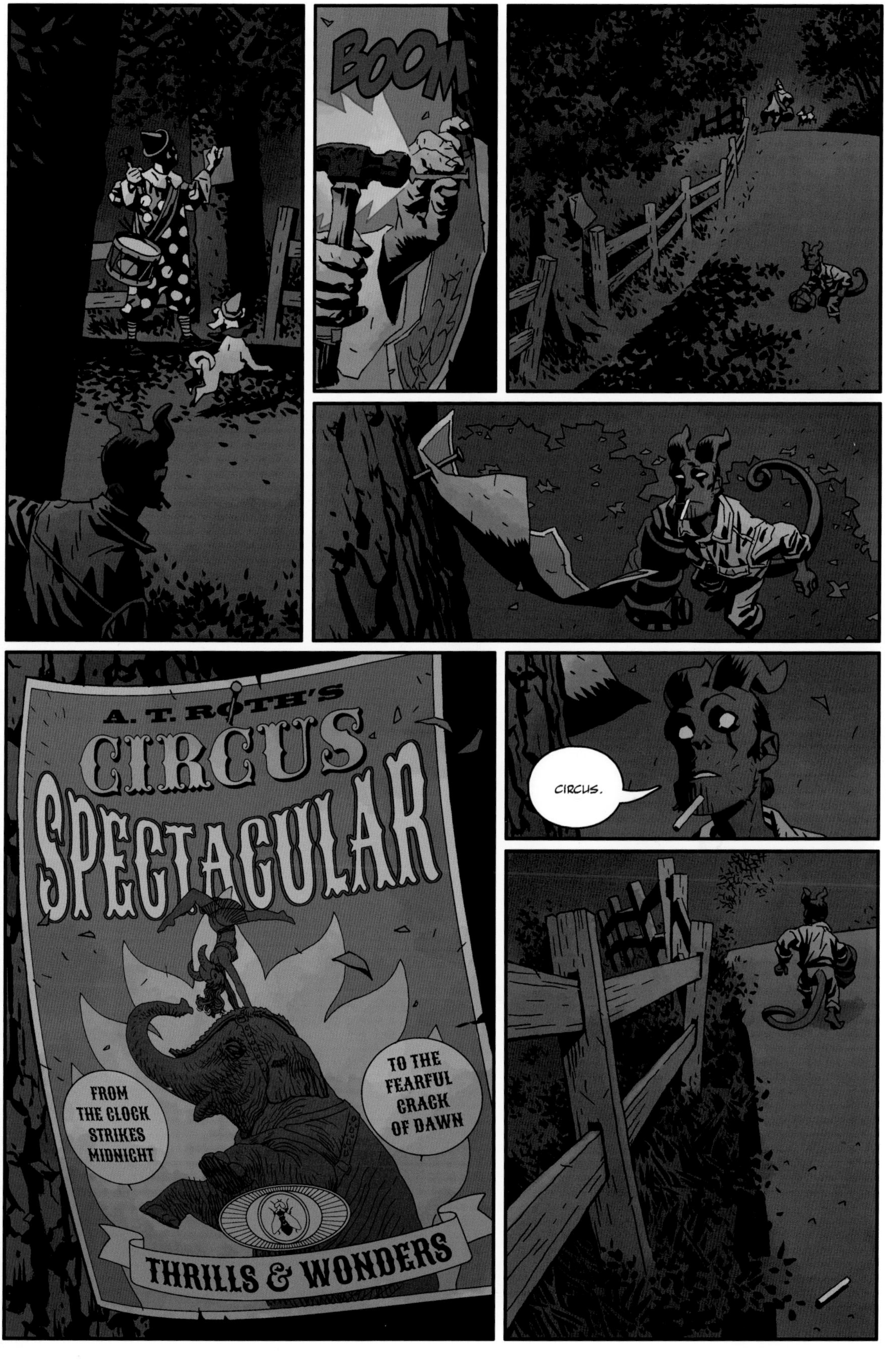
BOOM
A. T. ROTH'S
CIRCUS
SPECTACULAR
FROM THE CLOCK STRIKES MIDNIGHT
TO THE FEARFUL CRACK OF DAWN
THRILLS & WONDERS
CIRCUS.

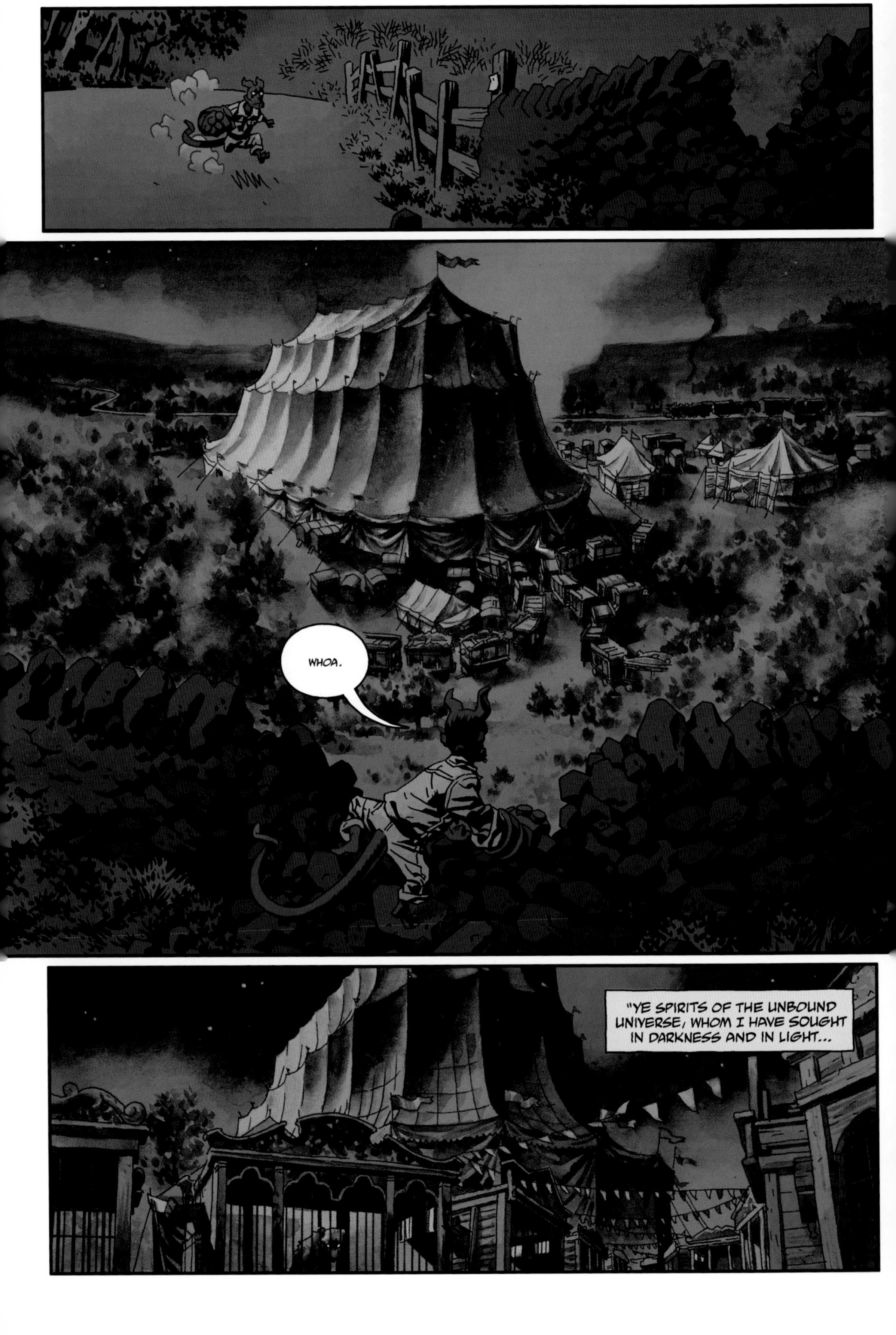
WHOA.
"YE SPIRITS OF THE UNBOUND UNIVERSE, WHOM I HAVE SOUGHT IN DARKNESS AND IN LIGHT...

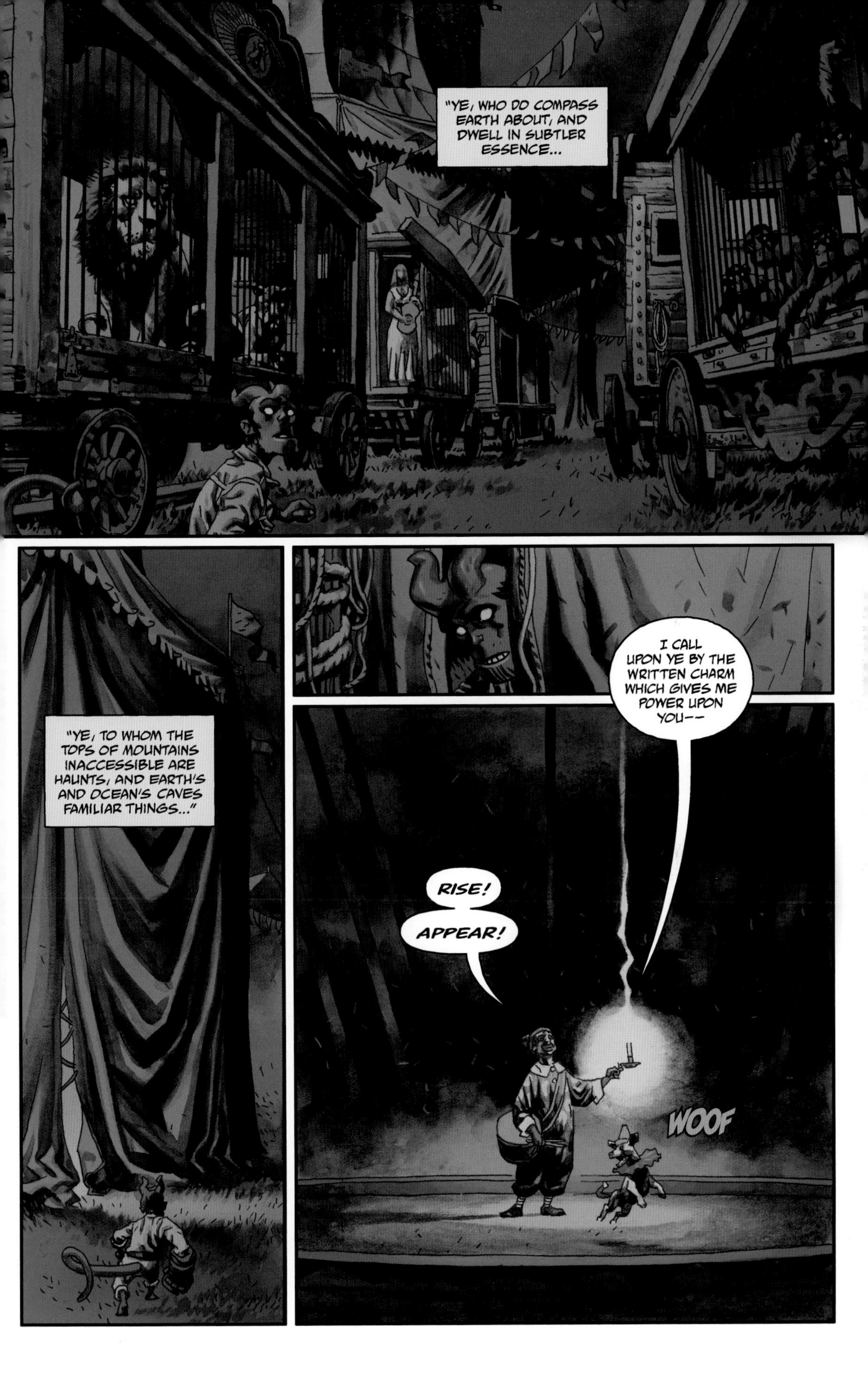
"YE, WHO DO COMPASS EARTH ABOUT, AND DWELL IN SUBTLER ESSENCE...
"YE, TO WHOM THE TOPS OF MOUNTAINS INACCESSIBLE ARE HAUNTS, AND EARTH'S AND OCEAN'S CAVES FAMILIAR THINGS..."
I CALL UPON YE BY THE WRITTEN CHARM WHICH GIVES ME POWER UPON YOU--
RISE!
APPEAR!
WOOF

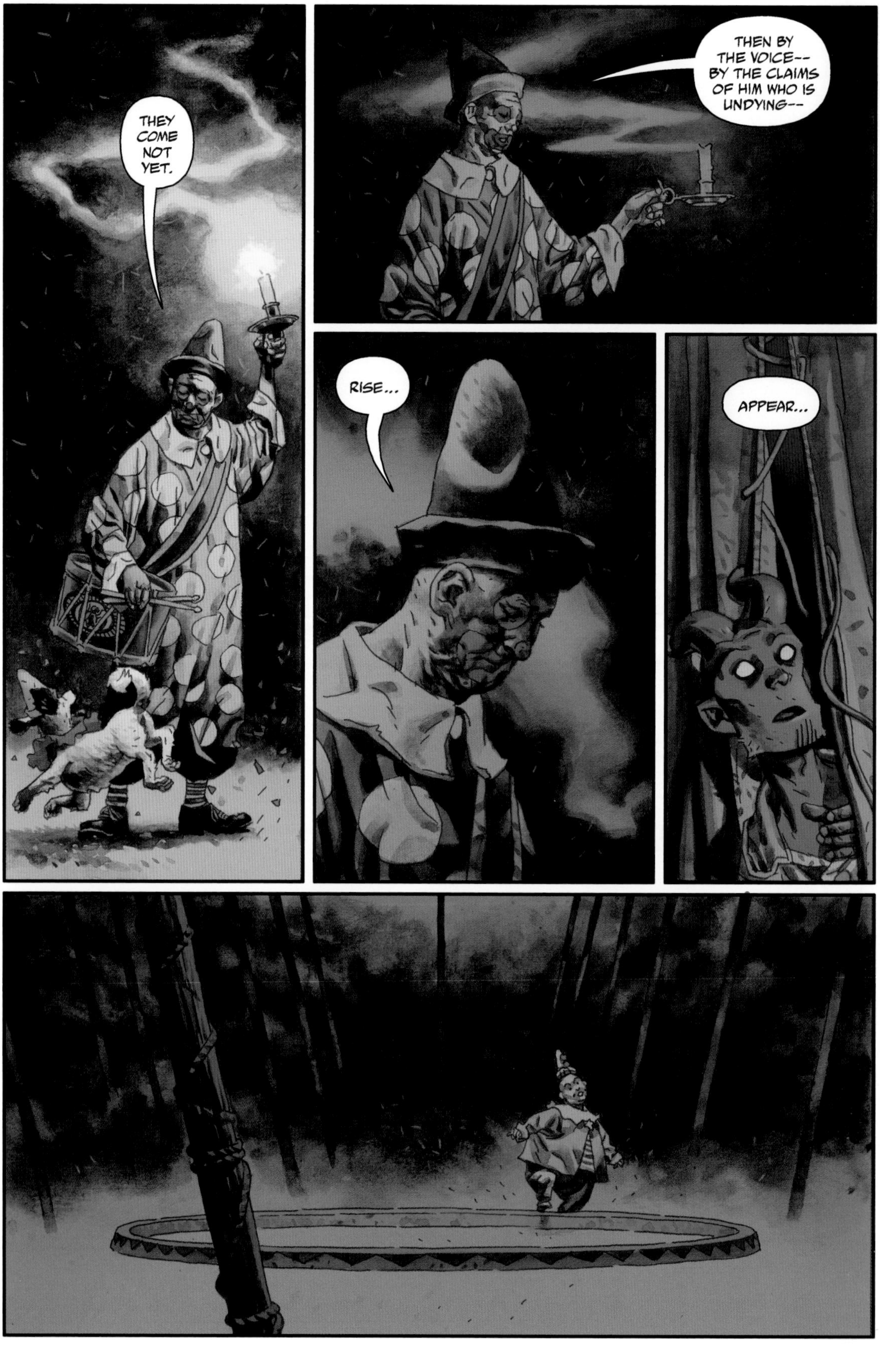
THEY COME NOT YET.
THEN BY THE VOICE-- BY THE CLAIMS OF HIM WHO IS UNDYING--
RISE...
APPEAR...

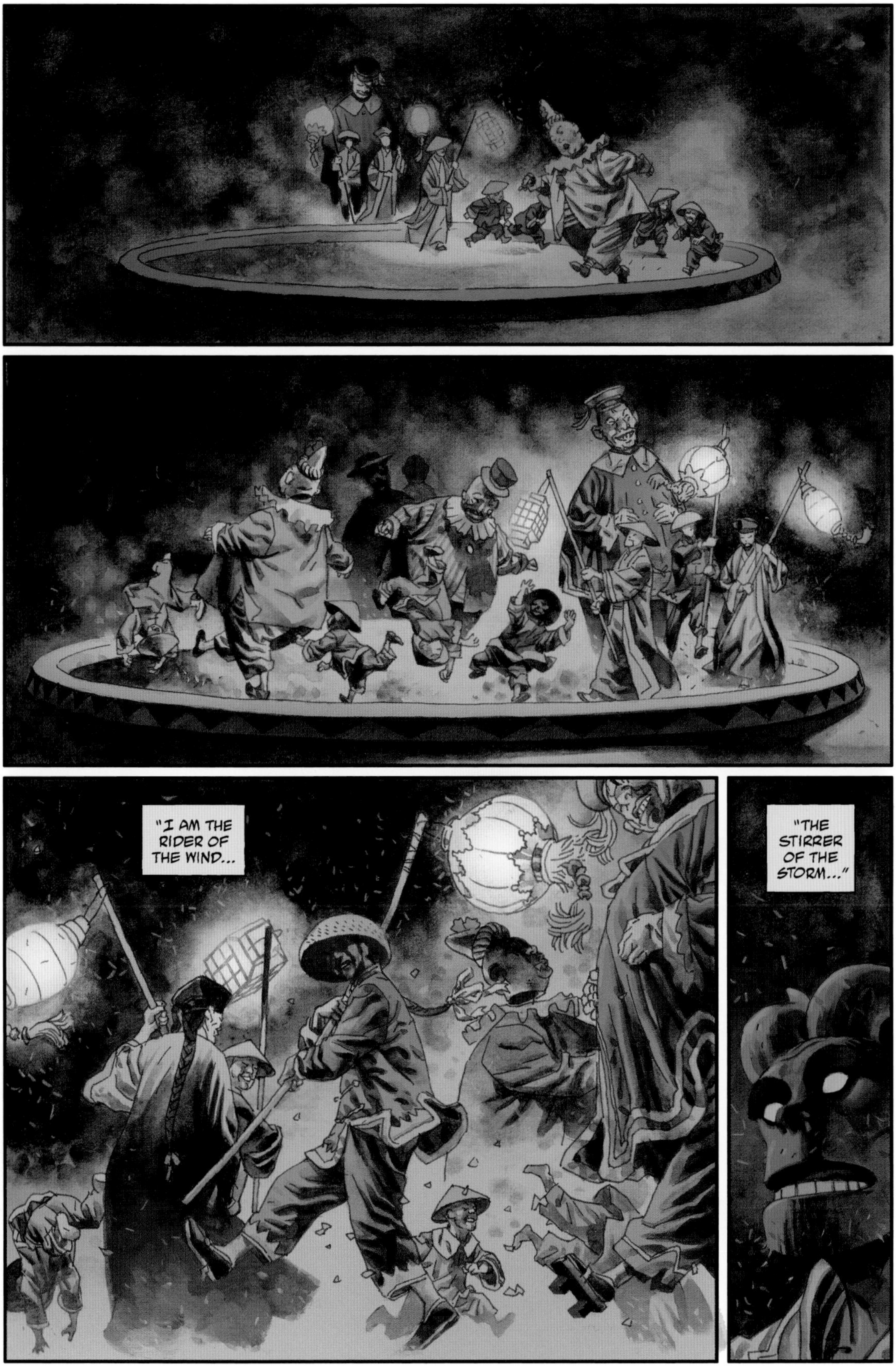
"I AM THE RIDER OF THE WIND...
"THE STIRRER OF THE STORM..."

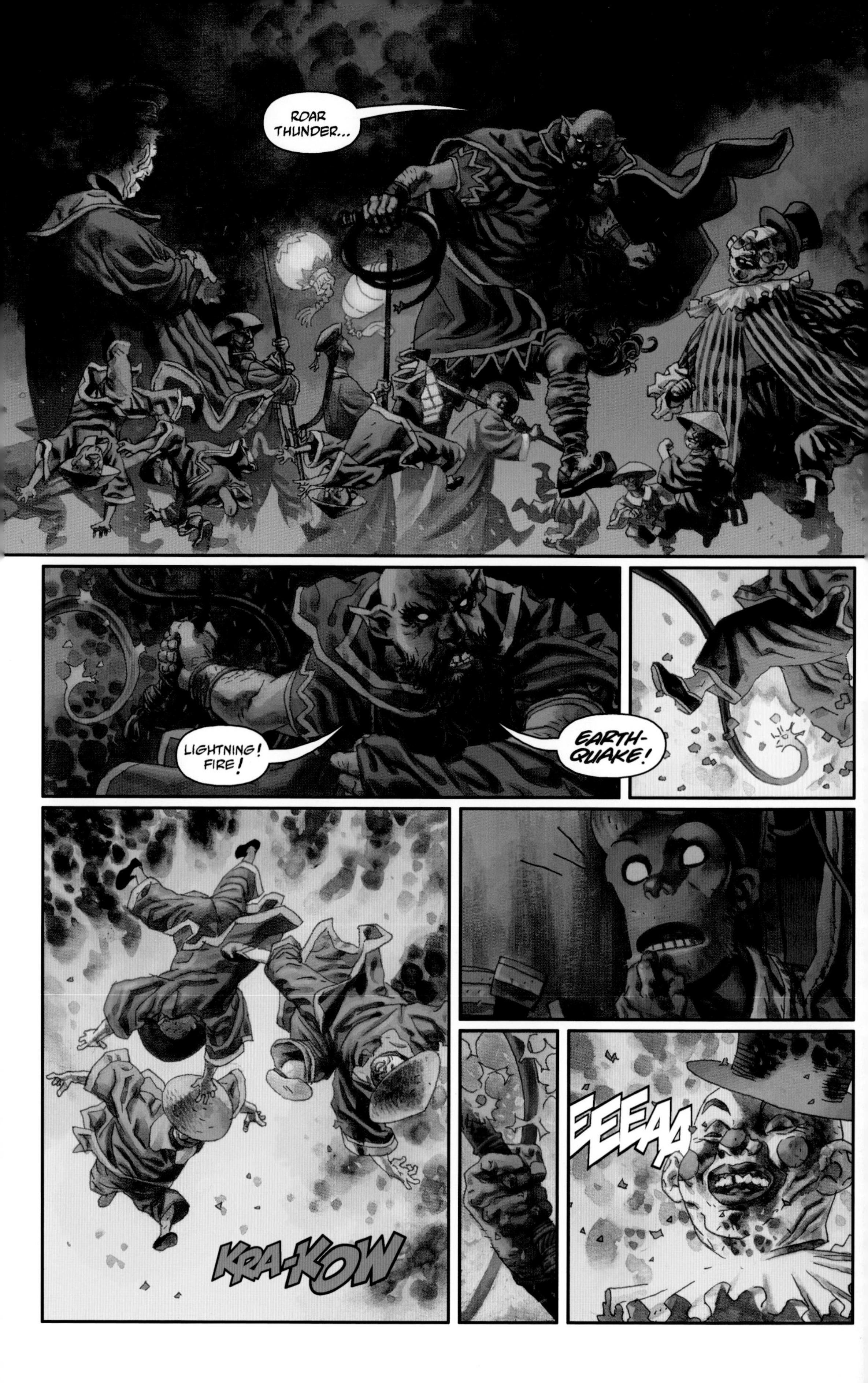

ROAR THUNDER...
LIGHTNING! FIRE!
EARTH-QUAKE!
KRA-KOW
EEEAA

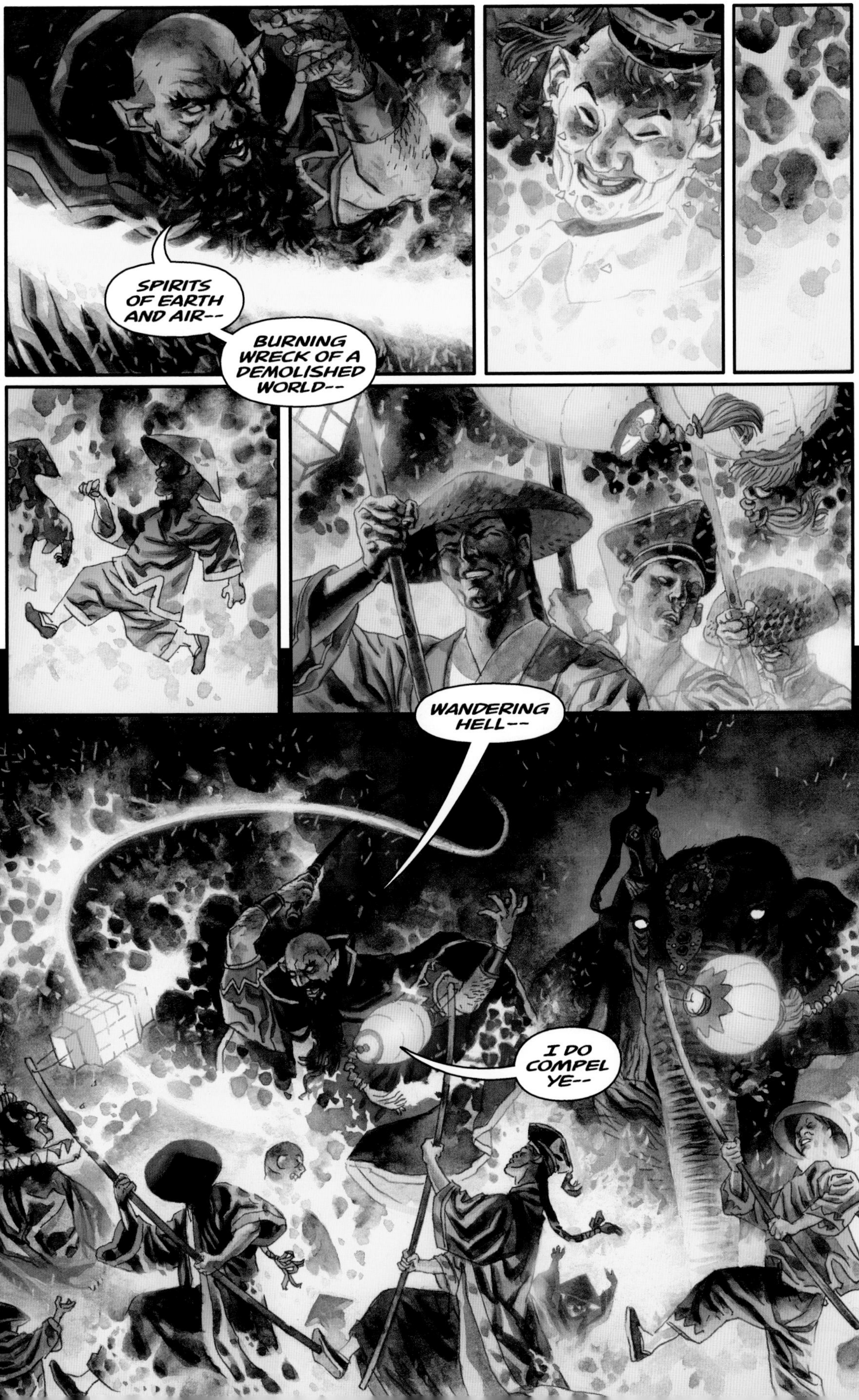
SPIRITS OF EARTH AND AIR--
BURNING WRECK OF A DEMOLISHED WORLD--
WANDERING HELL--
I DO COMPEL YE--

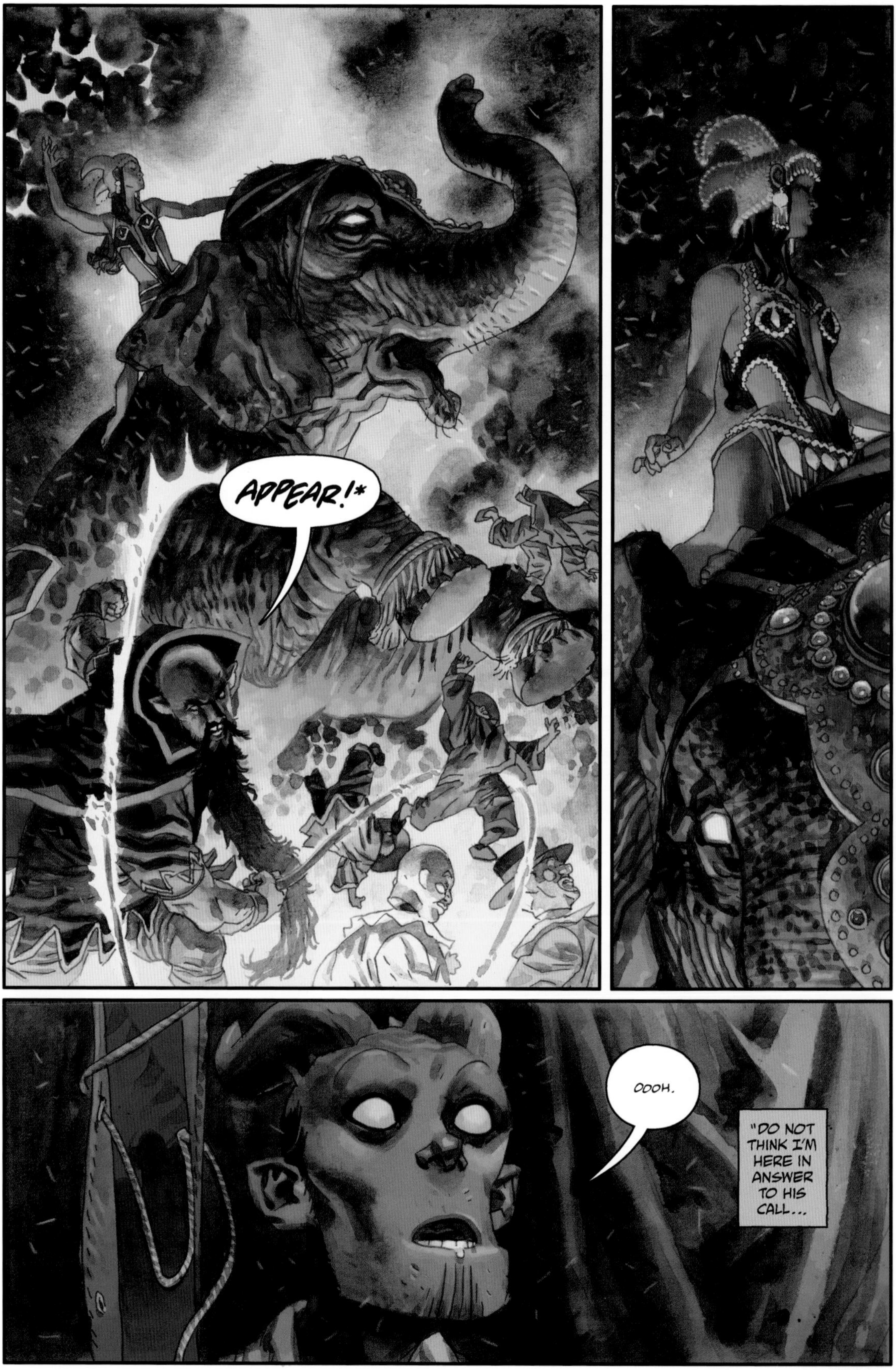
APPEAR!*
OOOH.
"DO NOT THINK I'M HERE IN ANSWER TO HIS CALL...

*CLOWN AND GIANT ARE RECITING (SORT OF) GEORGE GORDON, LORD BYRON'S **MANFRED**

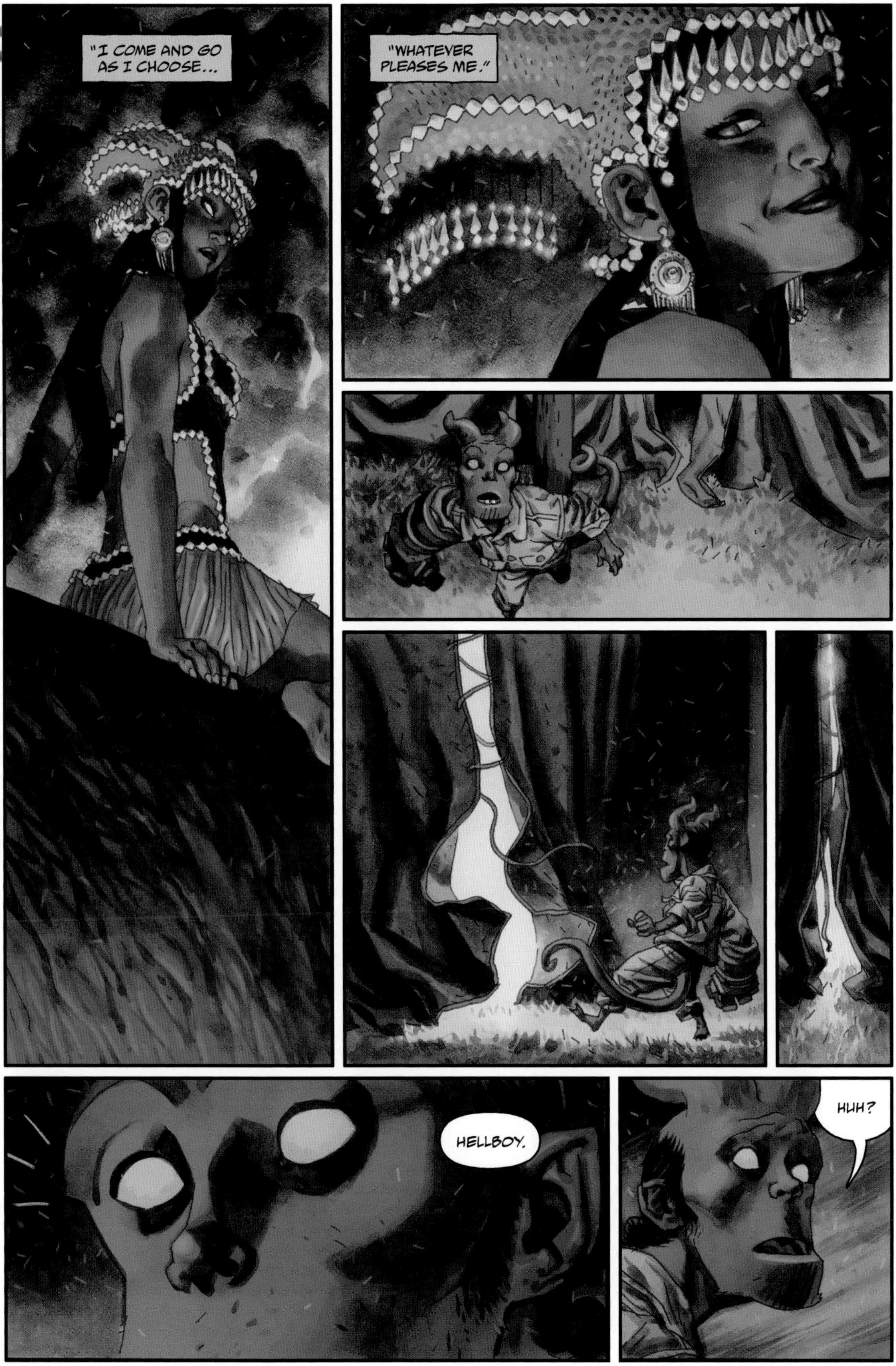
"I COME AND GO
AS I CHOOSE...
"WHATEVER
PLEASES ME."
HELLBOY.
HUH?

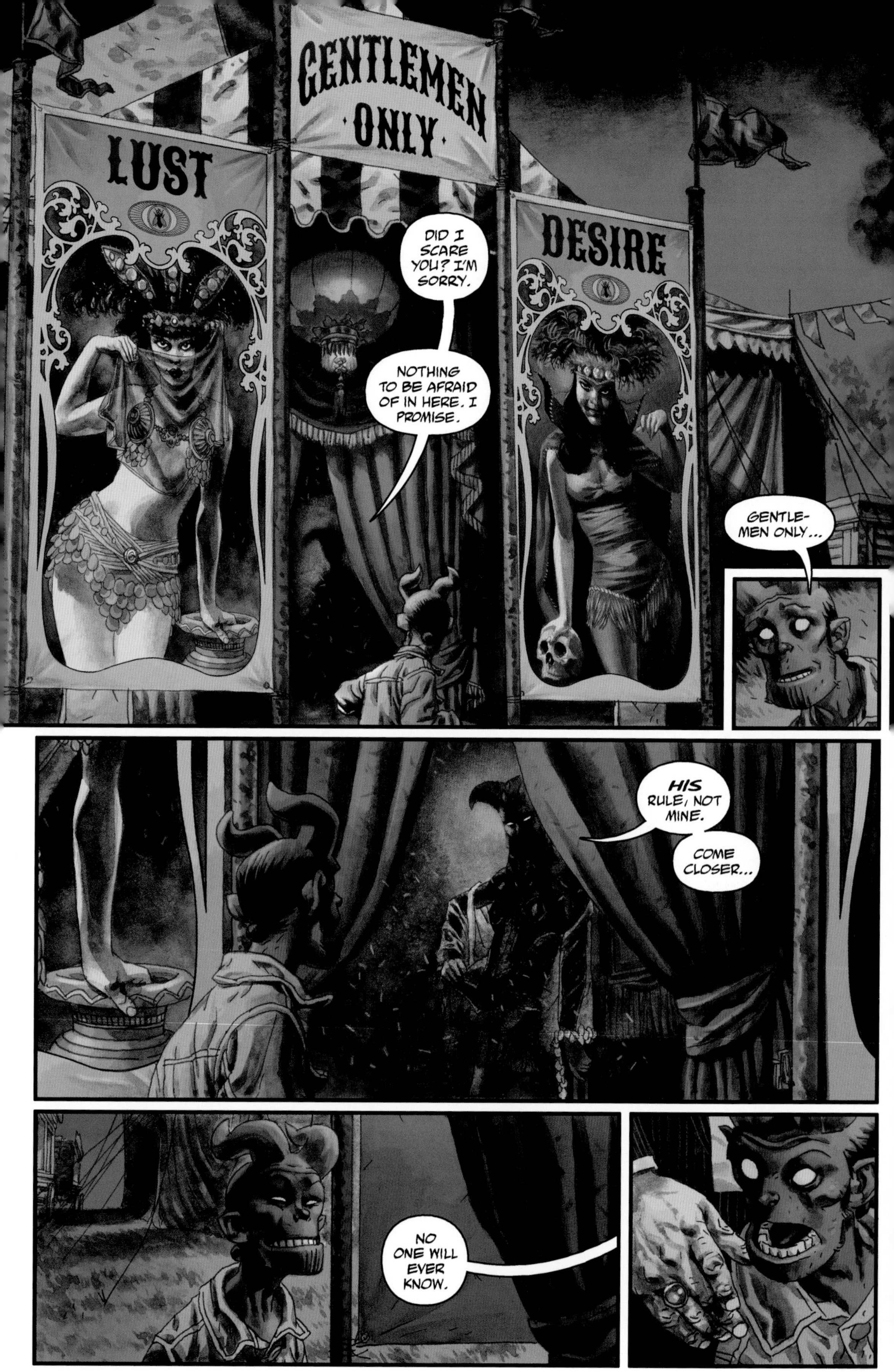
GENTLEMEN ONLY
LUST
DESIRE
DID I SCARE YOU? I'M SORRY.
NOTHING TO BE AFRAID OF IN HERE. I PROMISE.
GENTLE-MEN ONLY...
HIS RULE, NOT MINE.
COME CLOSER...
NO ONE WILL EVER KNOW.

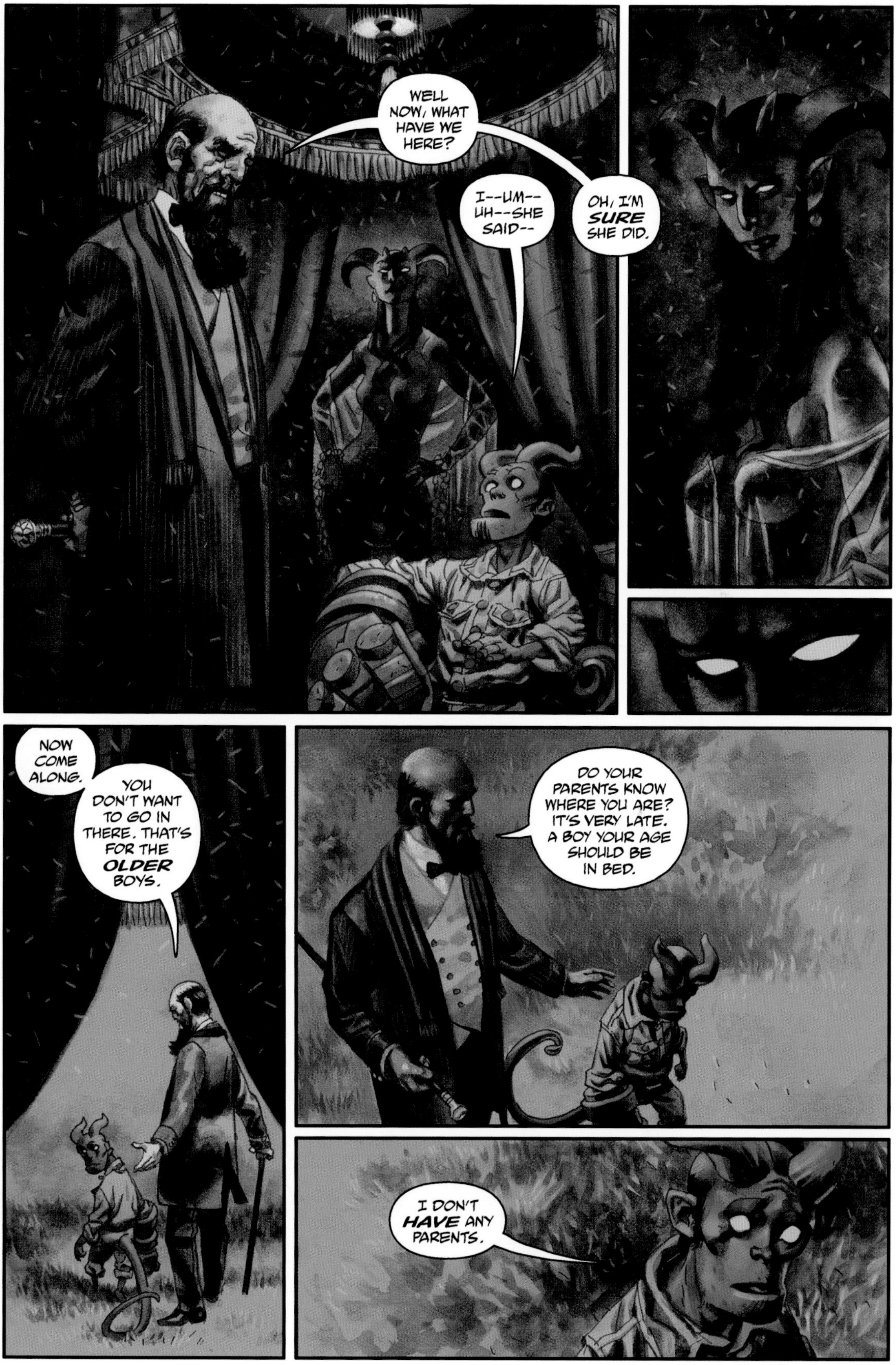
WELL NOW, WHAT HAVE WE HERE?
I--UM--UH--SHE SAID--
OH, I'M SURE SHE DID.
NOW COME ALONG.
YOU DON'T WANT TO GO IN THERE. THAT'S FOR THE OLDER BOYS.
DO YOUR PARENTS KNOW WHERE YOU ARE? IT'S VERY LATE. A BOY YOUR AGE SHOULD BE IN BED.
I DON'T HAVE ANY PARENTS.

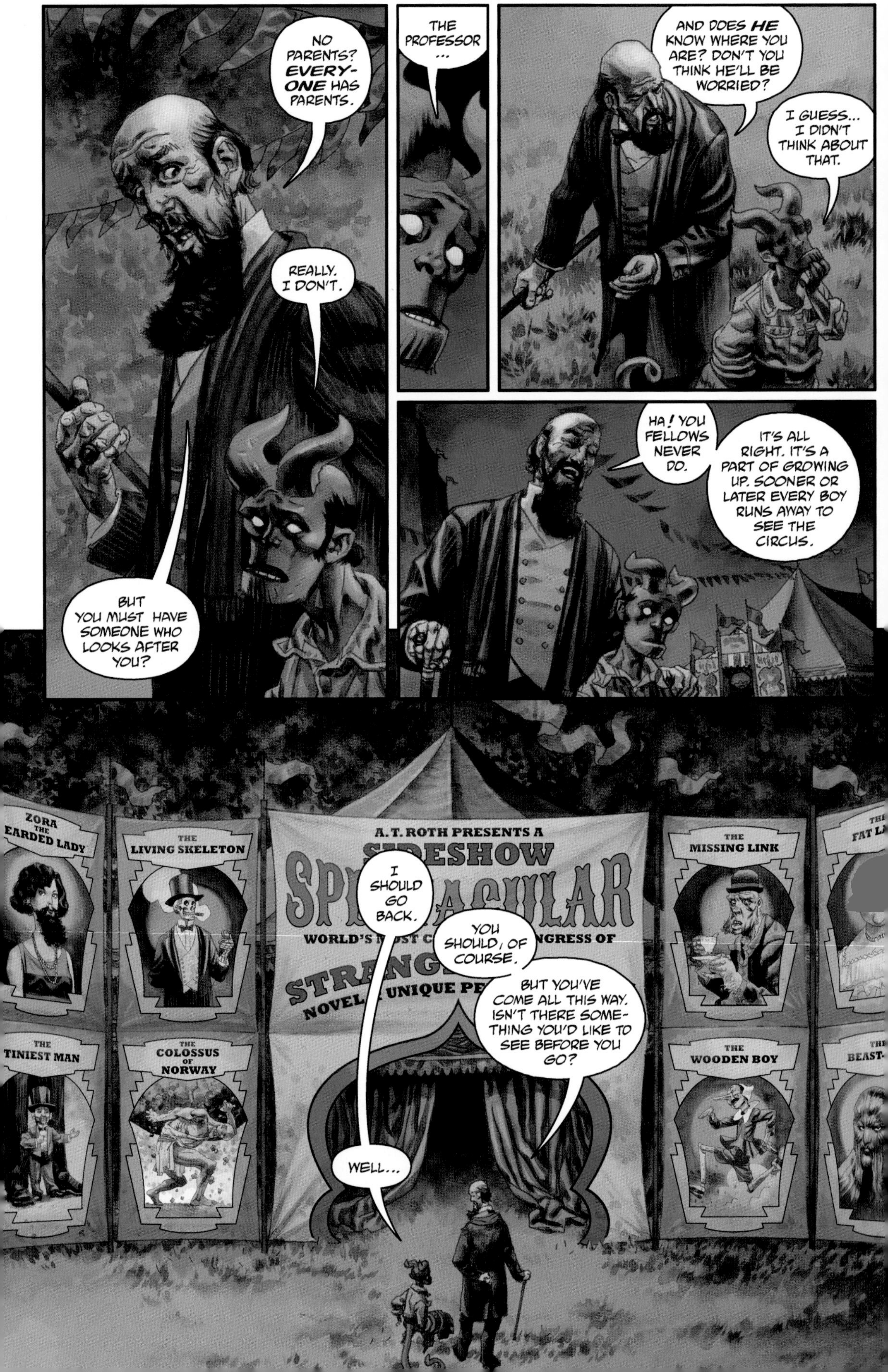

NO PARENTS? EVERY-ONE HAS PARENTS.
REALLY. I DON'T.
BUT YOU MUST HAVE SOMEONE WHO LOOKS AFTER YOU?
THE PROFESSOR ...
AND DOES HE KNOW WHERE YOU ARE? DON'T YOU THINK HE'LL BE WORRIED?
I GUESS... I DIDN'T THINK ABOUT THAT.
HA! YOU FELLOWS NEVER DO.
IT'S ALL RIGHT. IT'S A PART OF GROWING UP. SOONER OR LATER EVERY BOY RUNS AWAY TO SEE THE CIRCUS.
ZORA THE EARDED LADY
THE LIVING SKELETON
A. T. ROTH PRESENTS A
THE MISSING LINK
THE TINIEST MAN
THE COLOSSUS OF NORWAY
THE WOODEN BOY
I SHOULD GO BACK.
YOU SHOULD, OF COURSE.
BUT YOU'VE COME ALL THIS WAY. ISN'T THERE SOME-THING YOU'D LIKE TO SEE BEFORE YOU GO?
WELL...

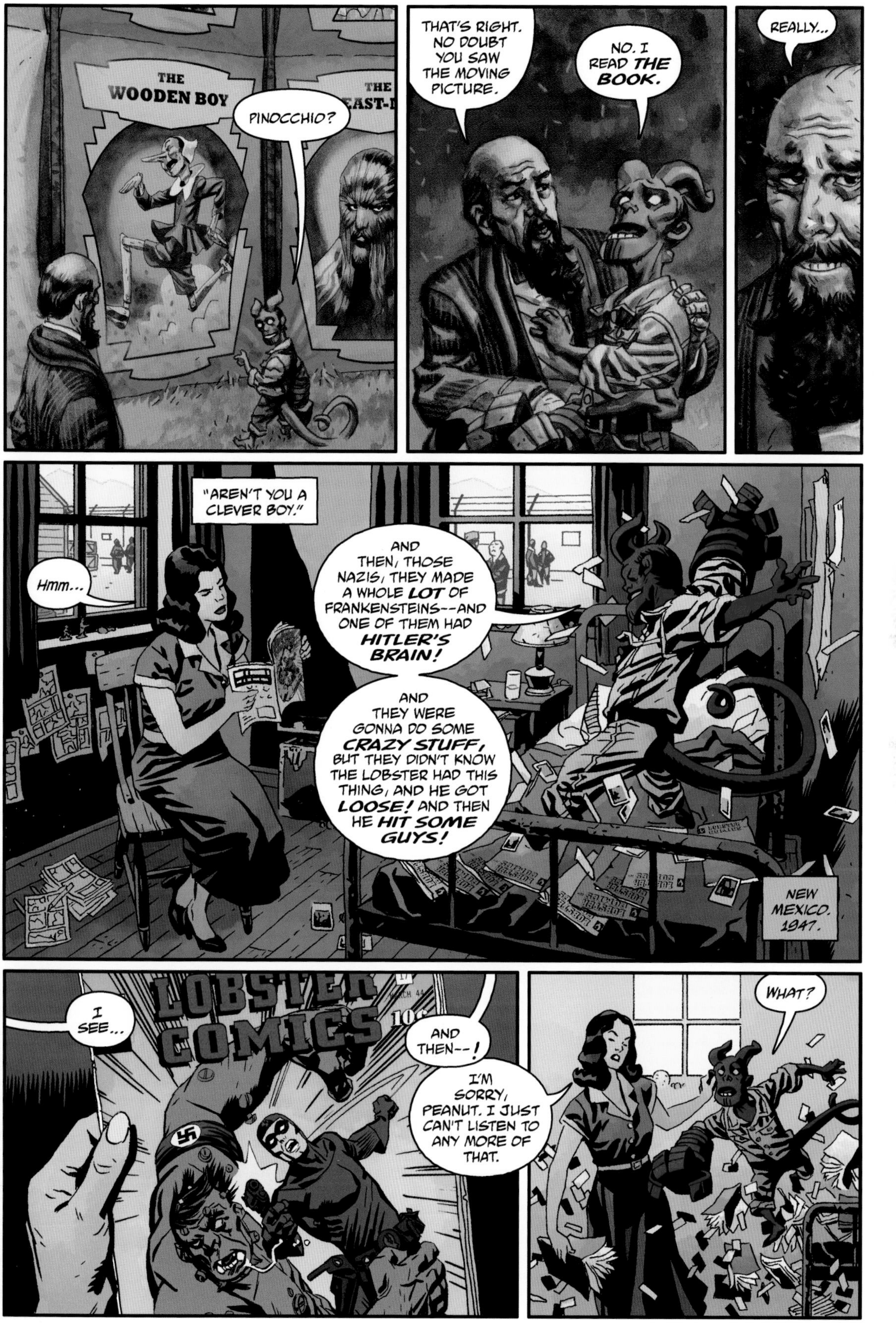
THE WOODEN BOY
PINOCCHIO?
THAT'S RIGHT. NO DOUBT YOU SAW THE MOVING PICTURE.
NO. I READ THE BOOK.
REALLY...
"AREN'T YOU A CLEVER BOY."
Hmm...
AND THEN, THOSE NAZIS, THEY MADE A WHOLE LOT OF FRANKENSTEINS--AND ONE OF THEM HAD HITLER'S BRAIN!
AND THEY WERE GONNA DO SOME CRAZY STUFF, BUT THEY DIDN'T KNOW THE LOBSTER HAD THIS THING, AND HE GOT LOOSE! AND THEN HE HIT SOME GUYS!
NEW MEXICO. 1947.
LOBSTER COMICS 10¢
I SEE...
AND THEN--!
I'M SORRY, PEANUT. I JUST CAN'T LISTEN TO ANY MORE OF THAT.
WHAT?

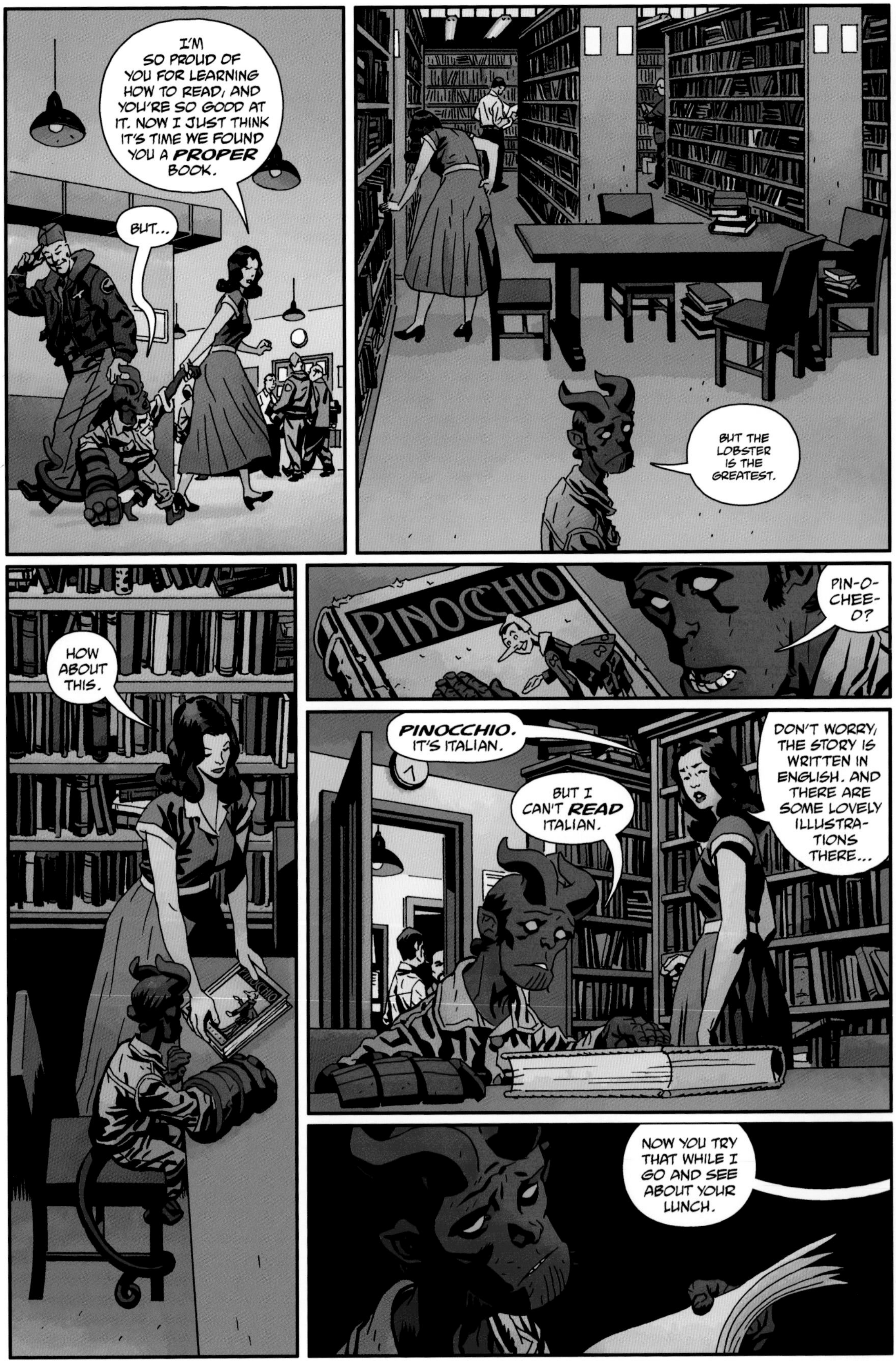

I'M SO PROUD OF YOU FOR LEARNING HOW TO READ, AND YOU'RE SO GOOD AT IT. NOW I JUST THINK IT'S TIME WE FOUND YOU A **PROPER** BOOK.
BUT...
BUT THE LOBSTER IS THE GREATEST.
HOW ABOUT THIS.
PINOCCHIO
PIN-O-CHEE-O?
PINOCCHIO. IT'S ITALIAN.
BUT I CAN'T ***READ*** ITALIAN.
DON'T WORRY, THE STORY IS WRITTEN IN ENGLISH. AND THERE ARE SOME LOVELY ILLUSTRATIONS THERE...
NOW YOU TRY THAT WHILE I GO AND SEE ABOUT YOUR LUNCH.

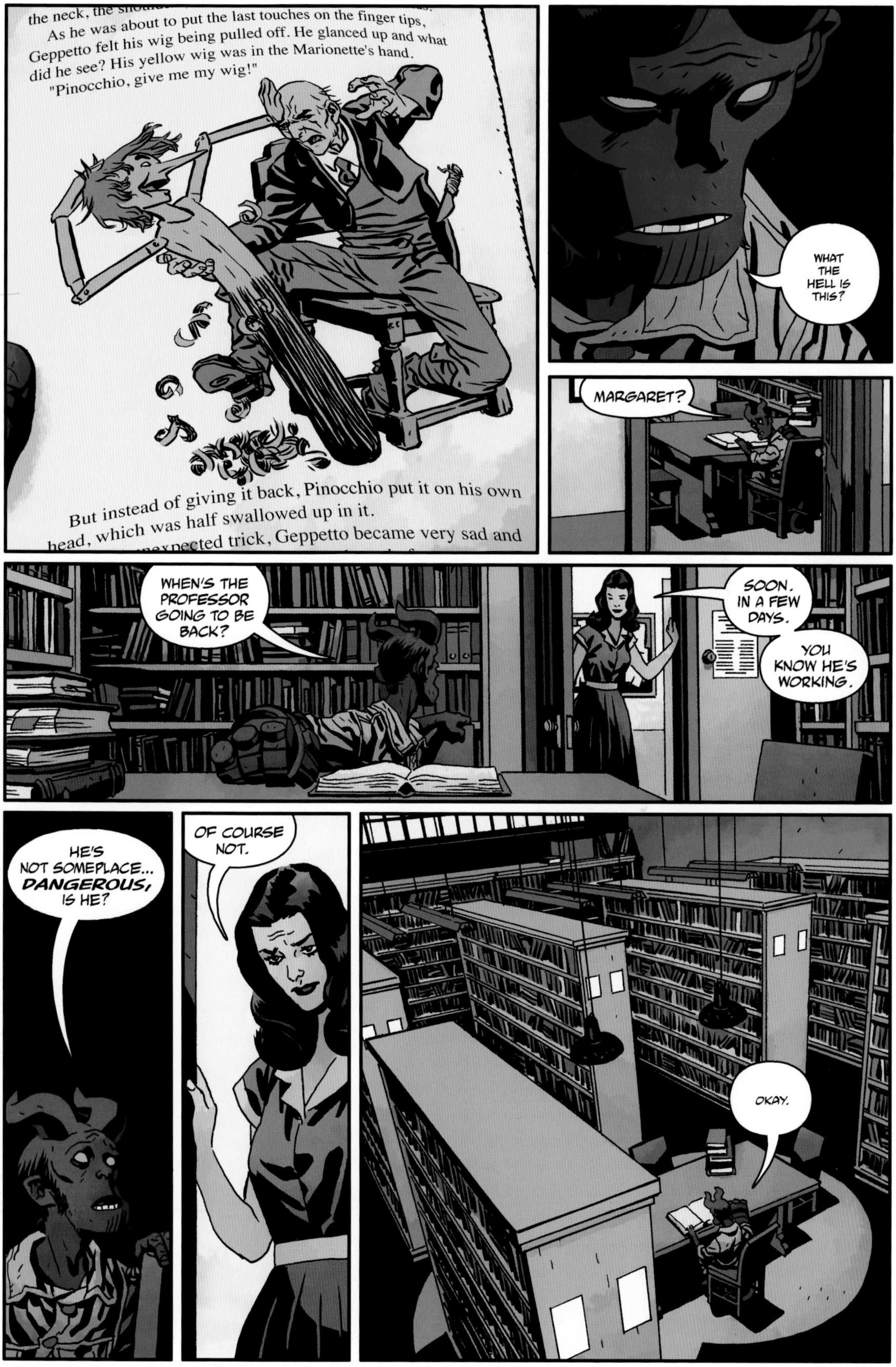

the neck, the
As he was about to put the last touches on the finger tips, Geppetto felt his wig being pulled off. He glanced up and what did he see? His yellow wig was in the Marionette's hand.
"Pinocchio, give me my wig!"
But instead of giving it back, Pinocchio put it on his own head, which was half swallowed up in it.
trick, Geppetto became very sad and
WHAT THE HELL IS THIS?
MARGARET?
WHEN'S THE PROFESSOR GOING TO BE BACK?
SOON. IN A FEW DAYS.
YOU KNOW HE'S WORKING.
HE'S NOT SOMEPLACE... ***DANGEROUS,*** IS HE?
OF COURSE NOT.
OKAY.

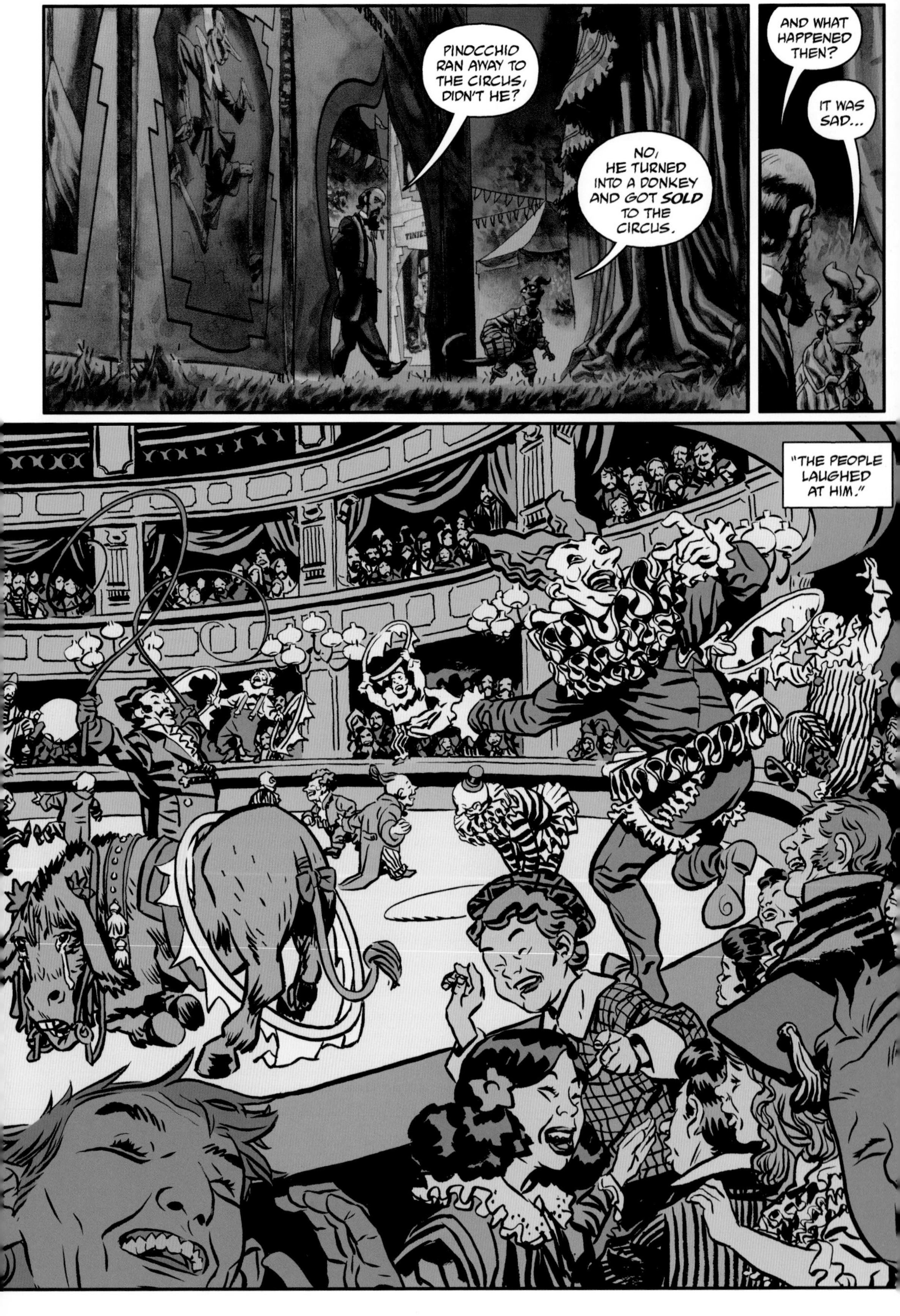
PINOCCHIO RAN AWAY TO THE CIRCUS, DIDN'T HE?
NO, HE TURNED INTO A DONKEY AND GOT **SOLD** TO THE CIRCUS.
AND WHAT HAPPENED THEN?
IT WAS SAD...
"THE PEOPLE LAUGHED AT HIM."

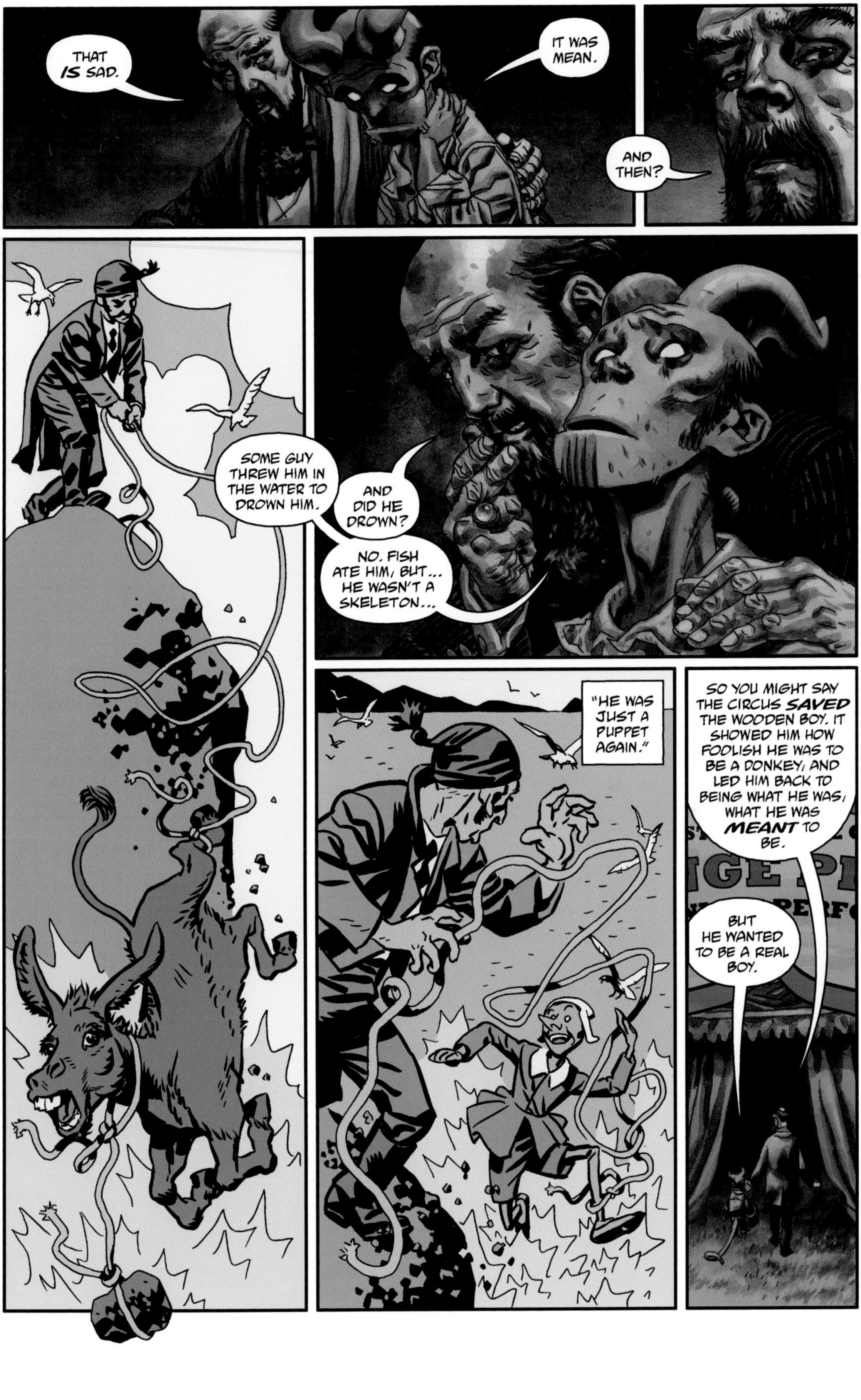

THAT IS SAD.
IT WAS MEAN.
AND THEN?
SOME GUY THREW HIM IN THE WATER TO DROWN HIM.
AND DID HE DROWN?
NO. FISH ATE HIM, BUT... HE WASN'T A SKELETON...
"HE WAS JUST A PUPPET AGAIN."
SO YOU MIGHT SAY THE CIRCUS SAVED THE WOODEN BOY. IT SHOWED HIM HOW FOOLISH HE WAS TO BE A DONKEY, AND LED HIM BACK TO BEING WHAT HE WAS, WHAT HE WAS MEANT TO BE.
BUT HE WANTED TO BE A REAL BOY.

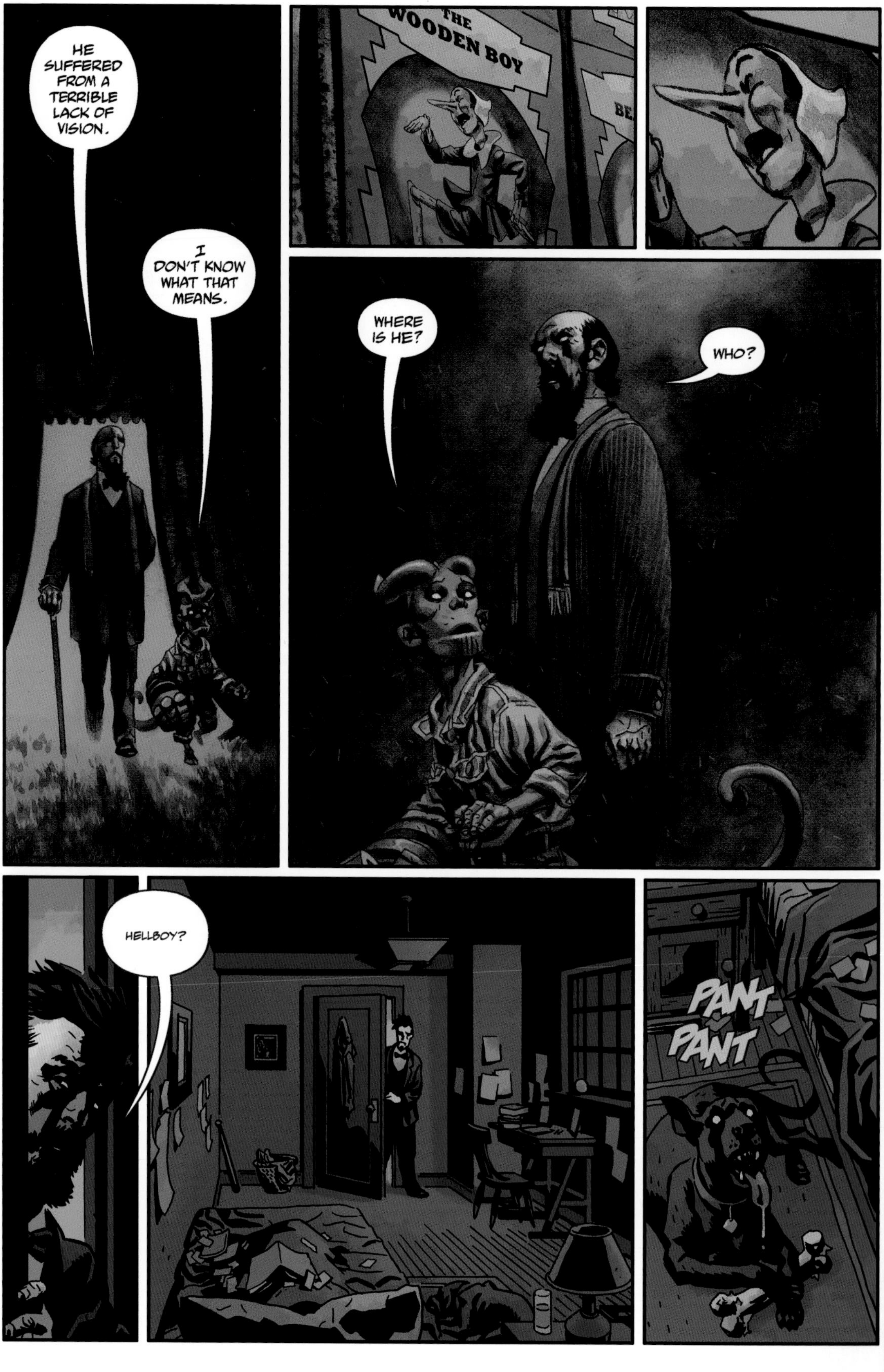
HE SUFFERED FROM A TERRIBLE LACK OF VISION.
I DON'T KNOW WHAT THAT MEANS.
THE WOODEN BOY
WHERE IS HE?
WHO?
HELLBOY?
PANT PANT

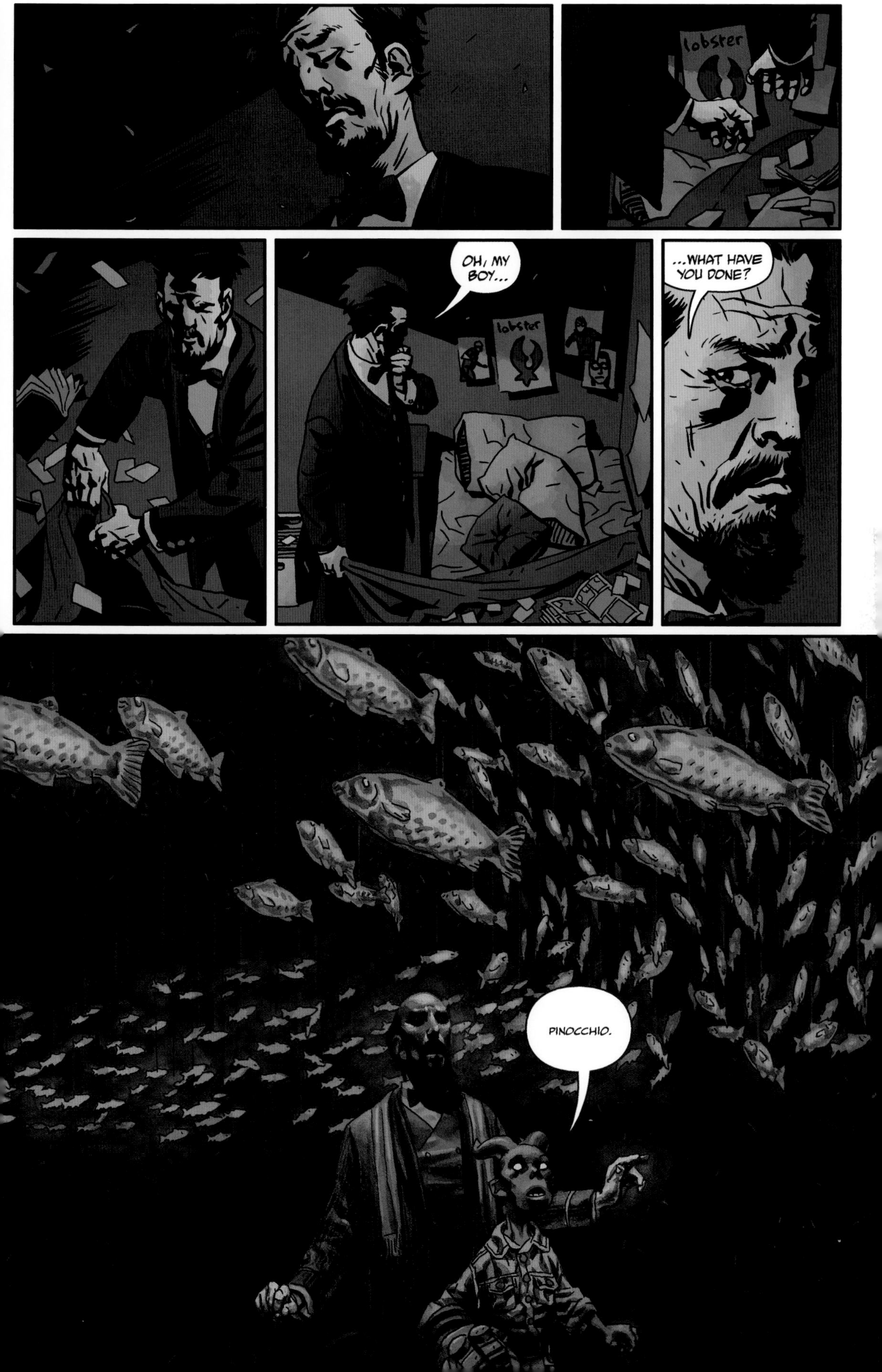
lobster
OH, MY BOY...
lobster
...WHAT HAVE YOU DONE?
PINOCCHIO.

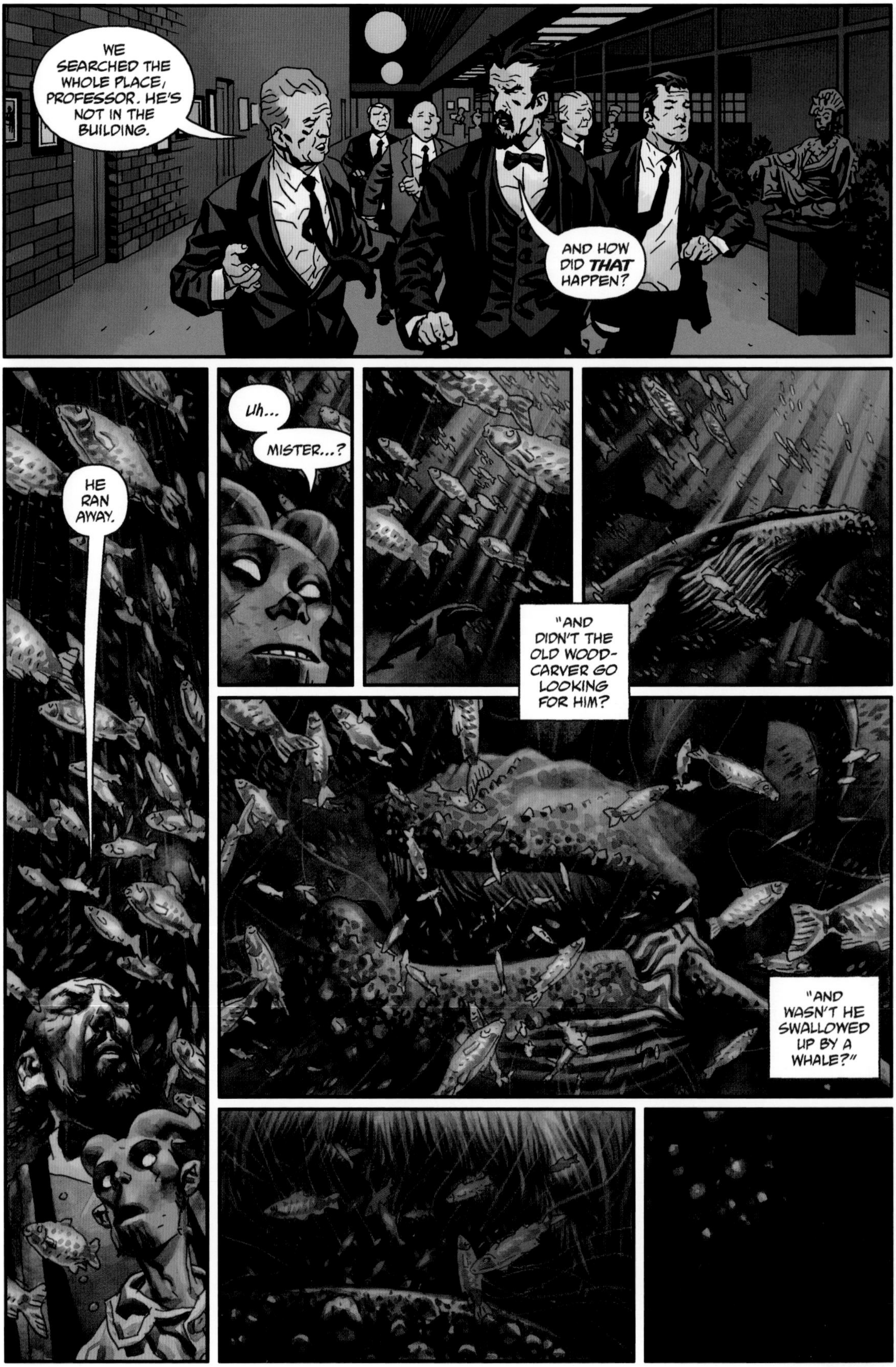
WE SEARCHED THE WHOLE PLACE, PROFESSOR. HE'S NOT IN THE BUILDING.
AND HOW DID **THAT** HAPPEN?
HE RAN AWAY.
Uh...
MISTER...?
"AND DIDN'T THE OLD WOOD-CARVER GO LOOKING FOR HIM?
"AND WASN'T HE SWALLOWED UP BY A WHALE?"

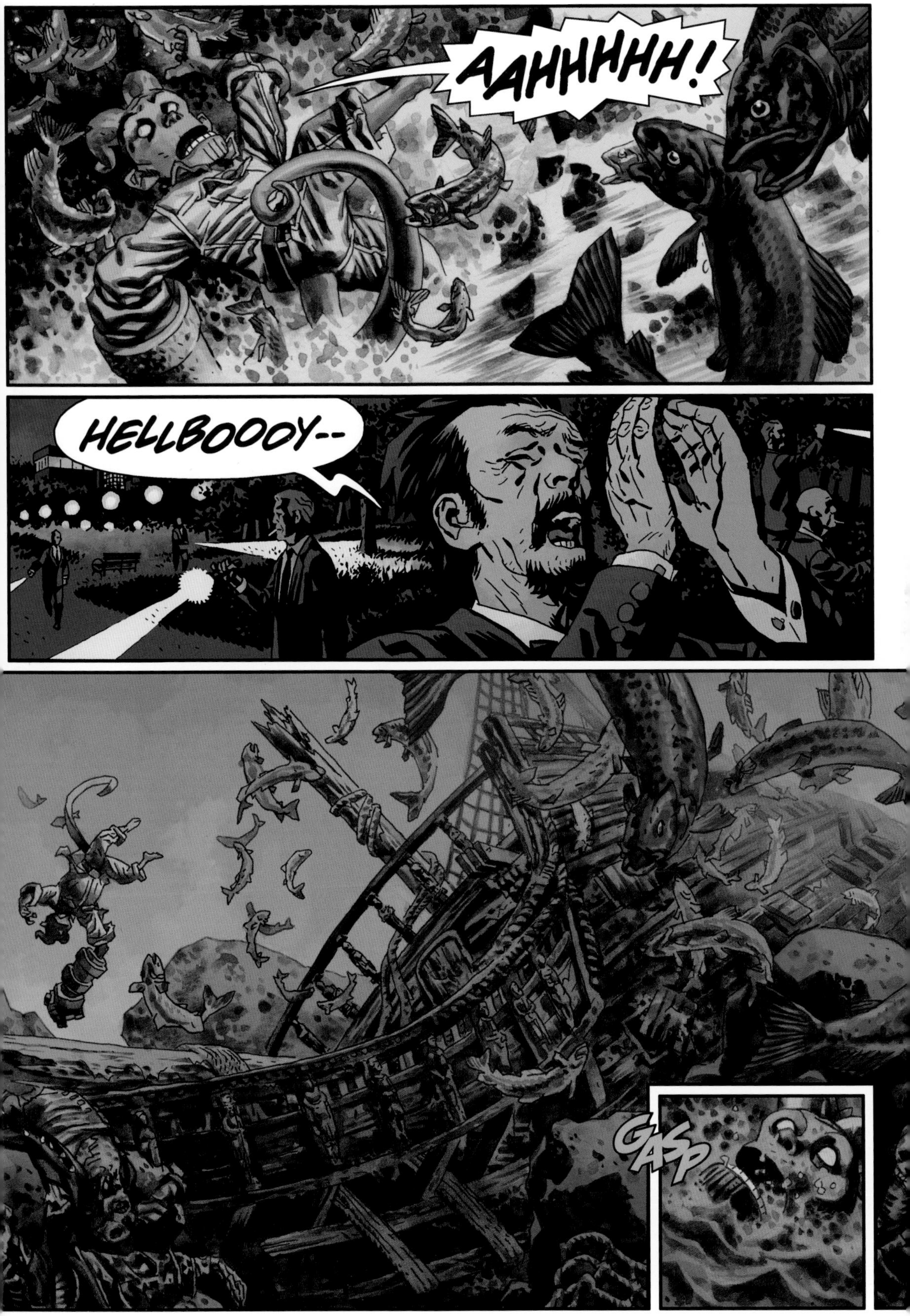
AAHHHHH!
HELLBOOOY--
GASP

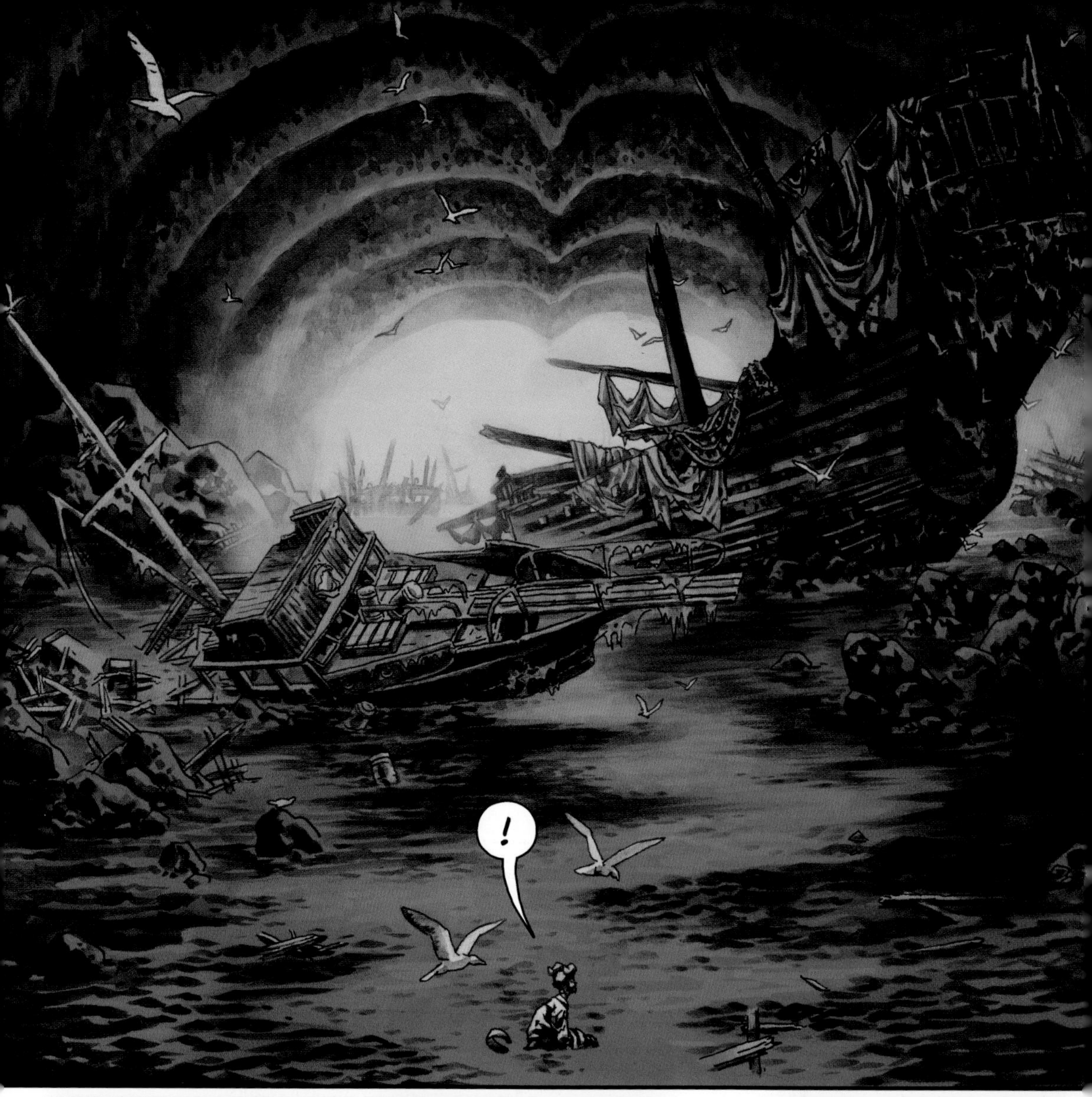
!

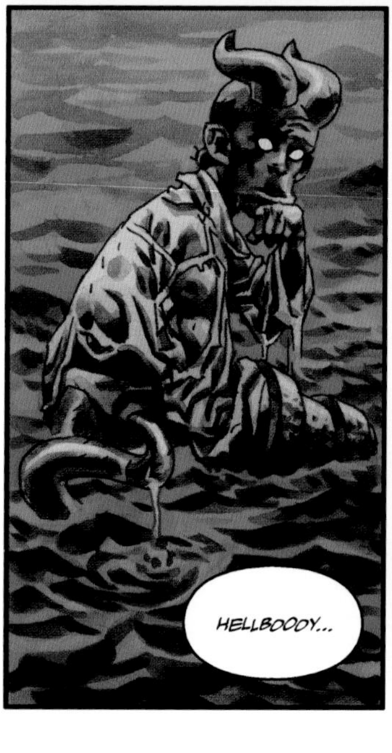
HELLBOOOY...

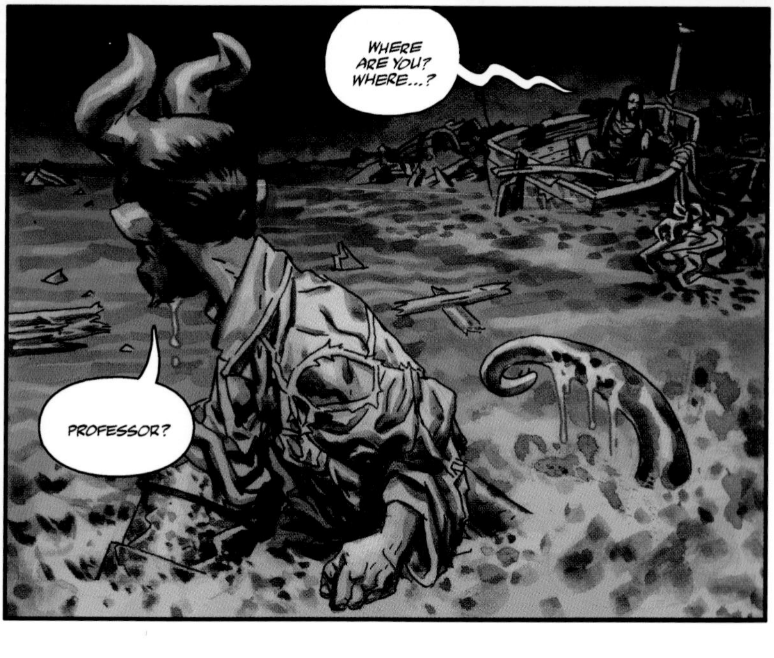
WHERE ARE YOU? WHERE...?
PROFESSOR?

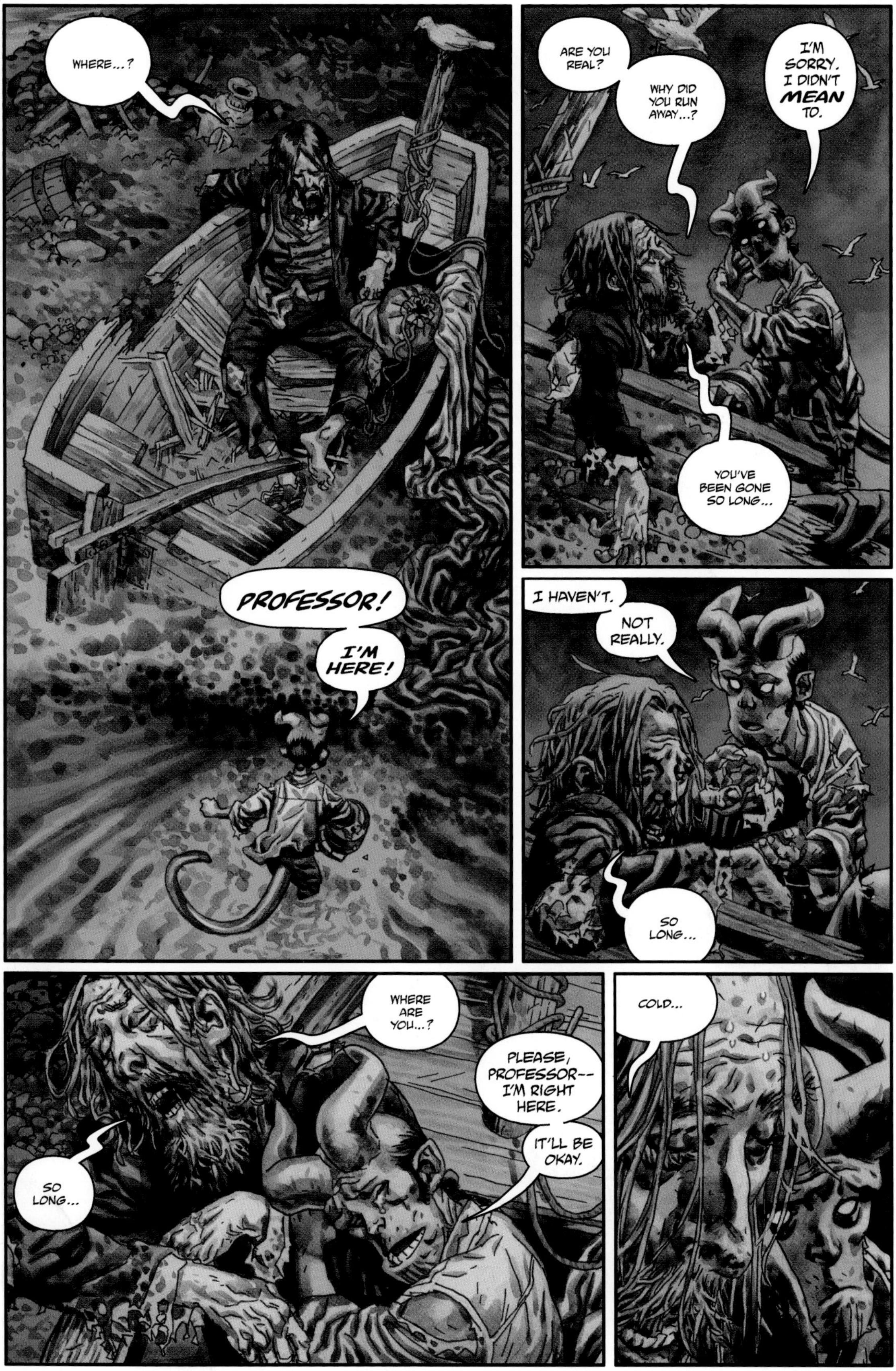
WHERE...?
PROFESSOR!
I'M HERE!
ARE YOU REAL?
WHY DID YOU RUN AWAY...?
I'M SORRY. I DIDN'T MEAN TO.
YOU'VE BEEN GONE SO LONG...
I HAVEN'T.
NOT REALLY.
SO LONG...
WHERE ARE YOU...?
SO LONG...
PLEASE, PROFESSOR-- I'M RIGHT HERE.
IT'LL BE OKAY.
COLD...

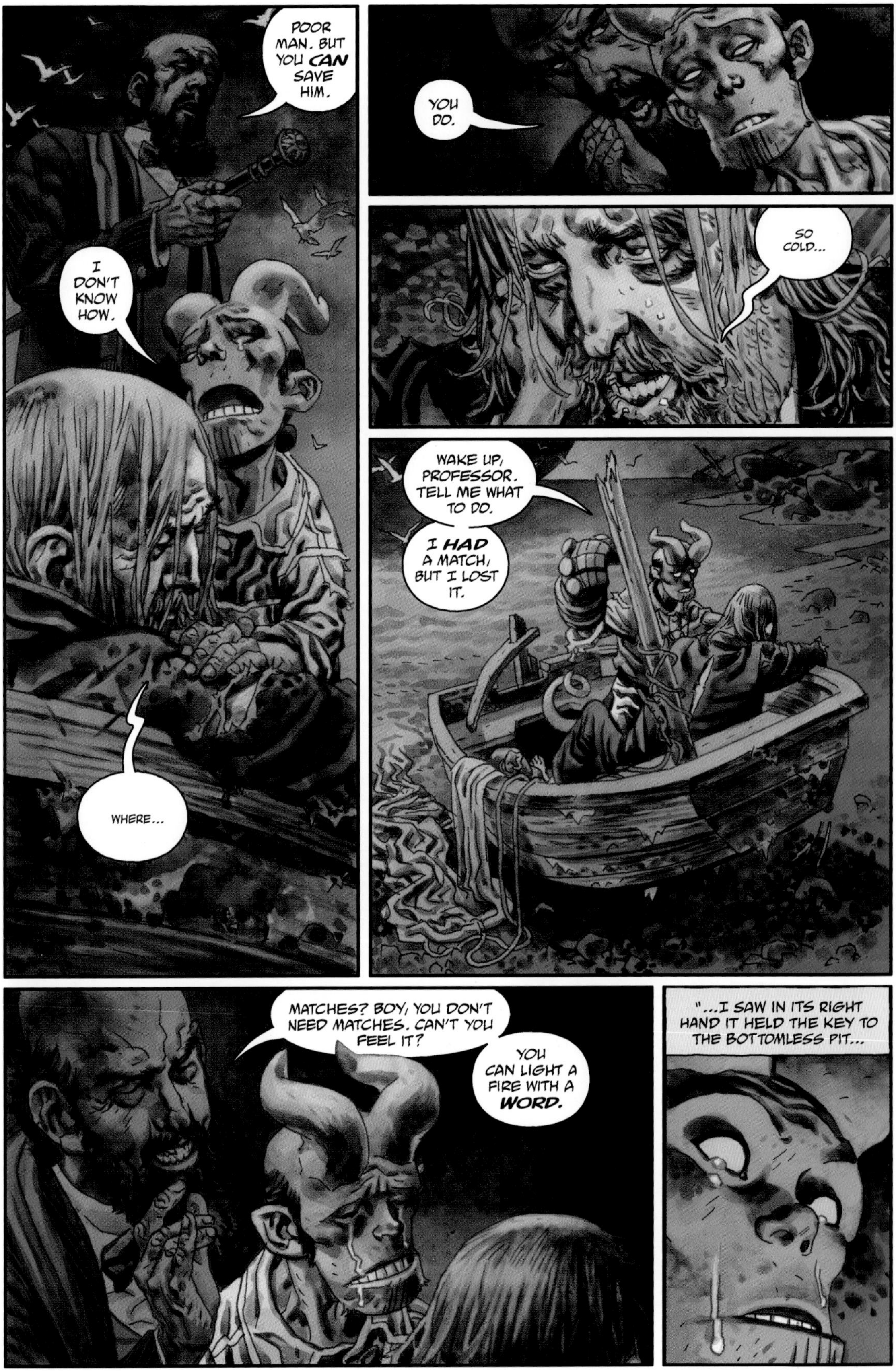
POOR MAN. BUT YOU CAN SAVE HIM.
I DON'T KNOW HOW.
WHERE...
YOU DO.
SO COLD...
WAKE UP, PROFESSOR. TELL ME WHAT TO DO.
I HAD A MATCH, BUT I LOST IT.
MATCHES? BOY, YOU DON'T NEED MATCHES. CAN'T YOU FEEL IT?
YOU CAN LIGHT A FIRE WITH A WORD.
"...I SAW IN ITS RIGHT HAND IT HELD THE KEY TO THE BOTTOMLESS PIT...

"AND I SAW A GREAT FIRE COME OUT OF IT, OUT OF THE DEPTHS OF HELL, AND ROAR ACROSS THE WHOLE FACE OF THE EARTH..."

NO!

COLD... HELLBOY... FREEZING...

WHY?

"AND AFTER THAT ONLY DARKNESS..."

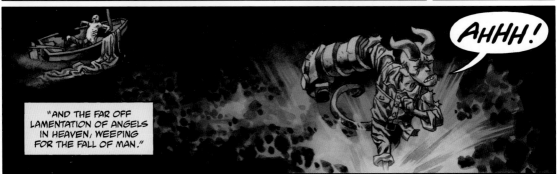

"AND THE FAR OFF LAMENTATION OF ANGELS IN HEAVEN, WEEPING FOR THE FALL OF MAN."

AHHH!

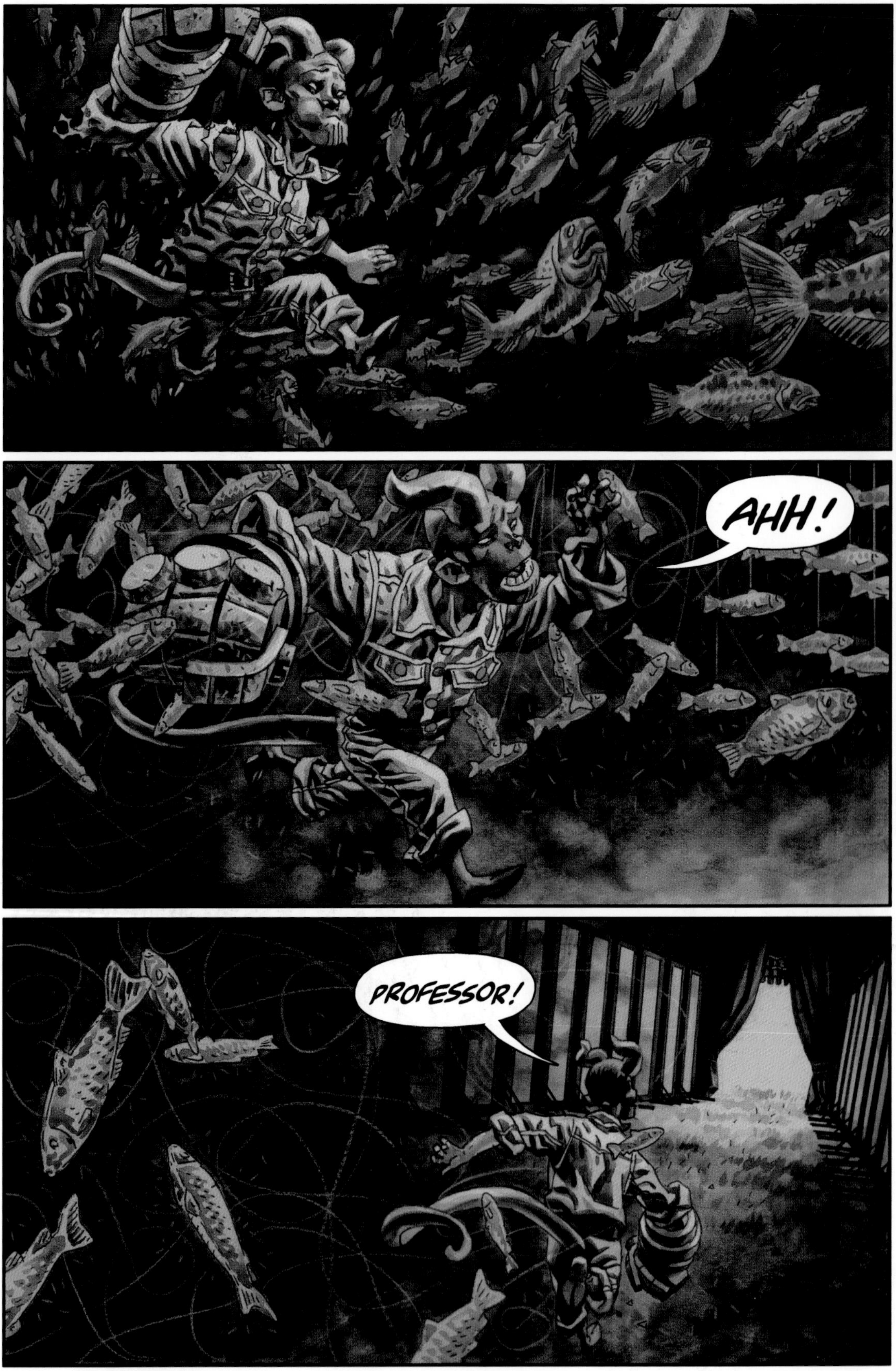
AHH!
PROFESSOR!

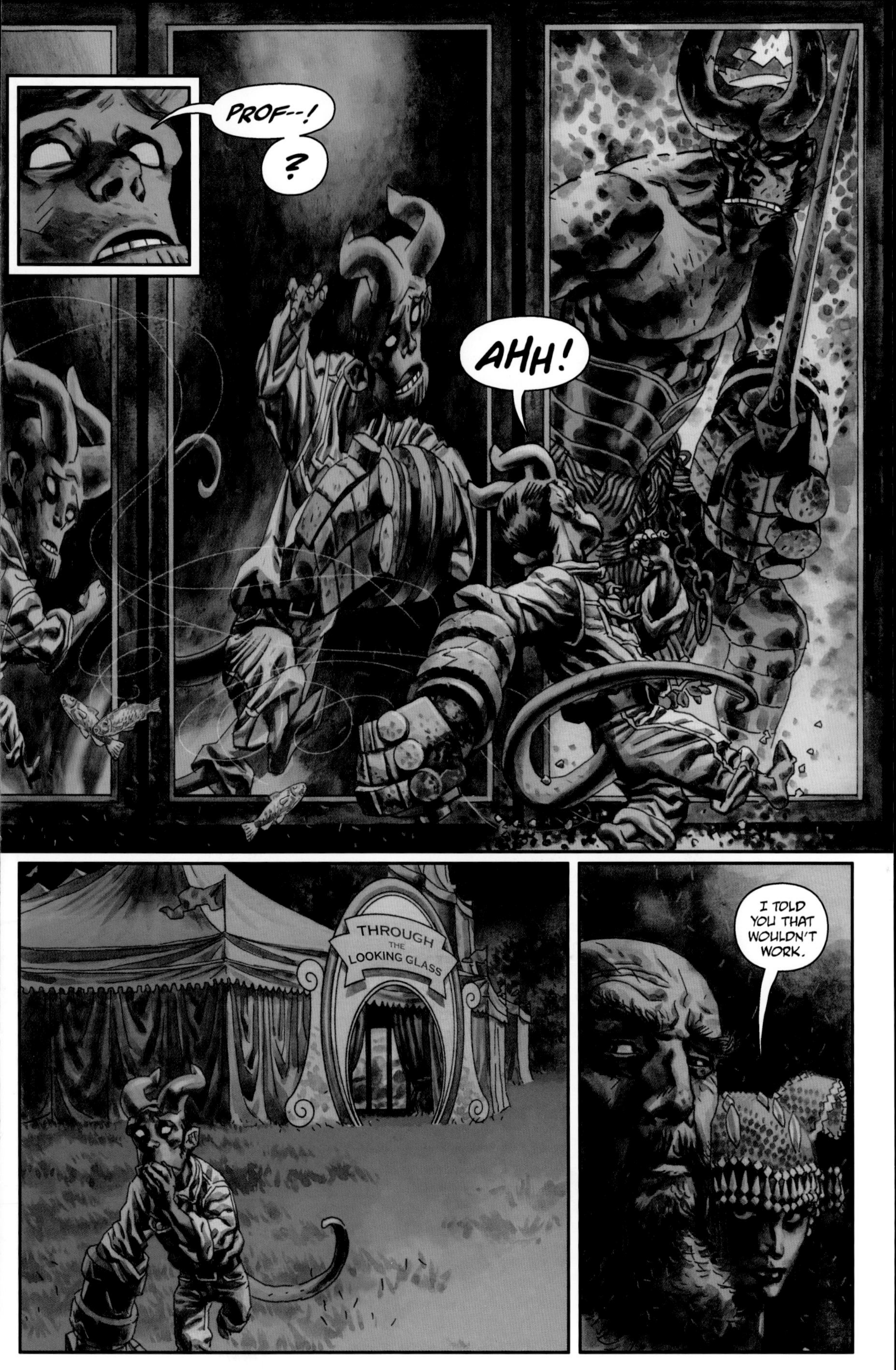
PROF--!
?
AHH!
THROUGH THE LOOKING GLASS
I TOLD YOU THAT WOULDN'T WORK.

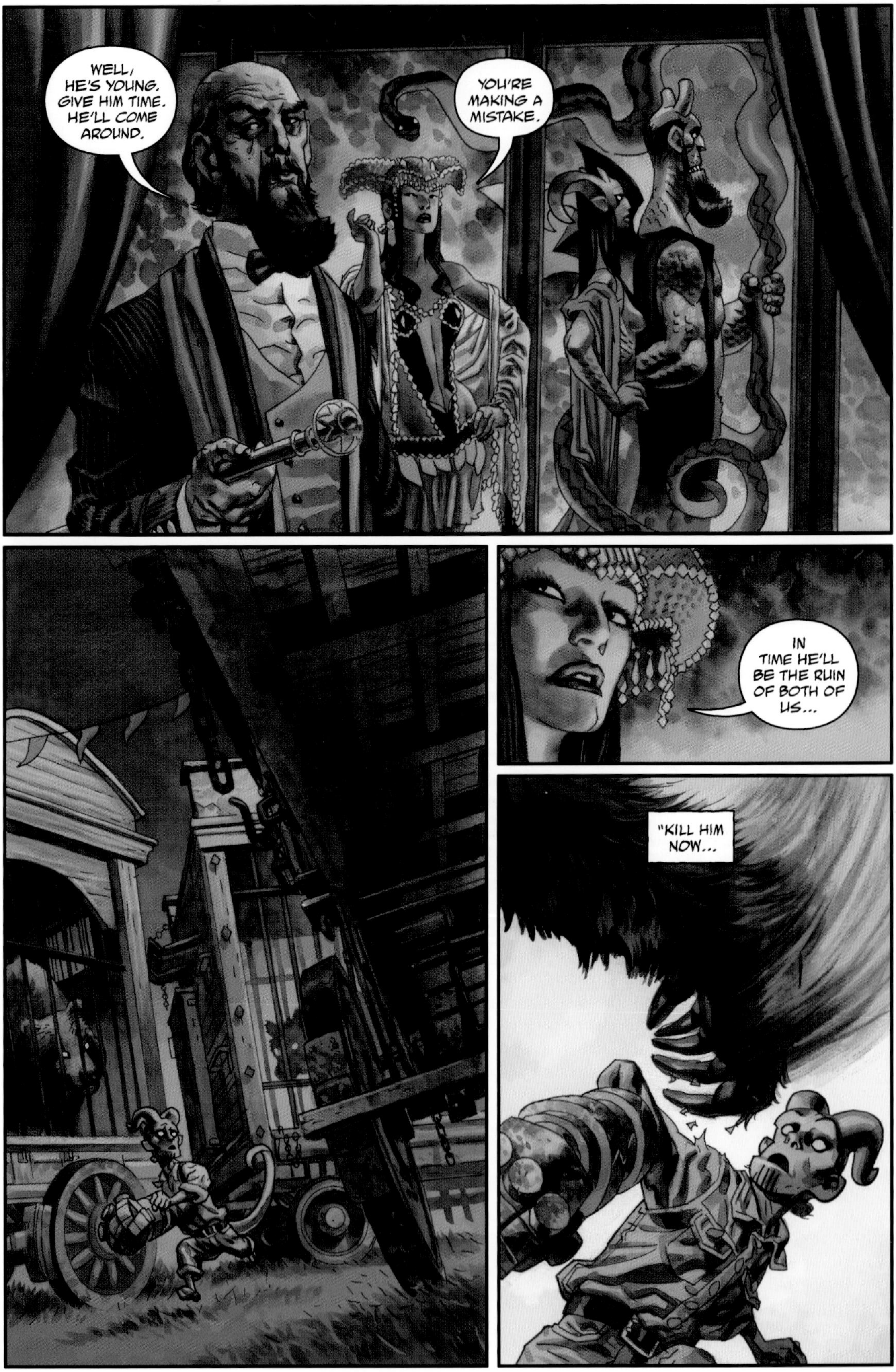
WELL, HE'S YOUNG. GIVE HIM TIME. HE'LL COME AROUND.
YOU'RE MAKING A MISTAKE.
IN TIME HE'LL BE THE RUIN OF BOTH OF US...
"KILL HIM NOW...

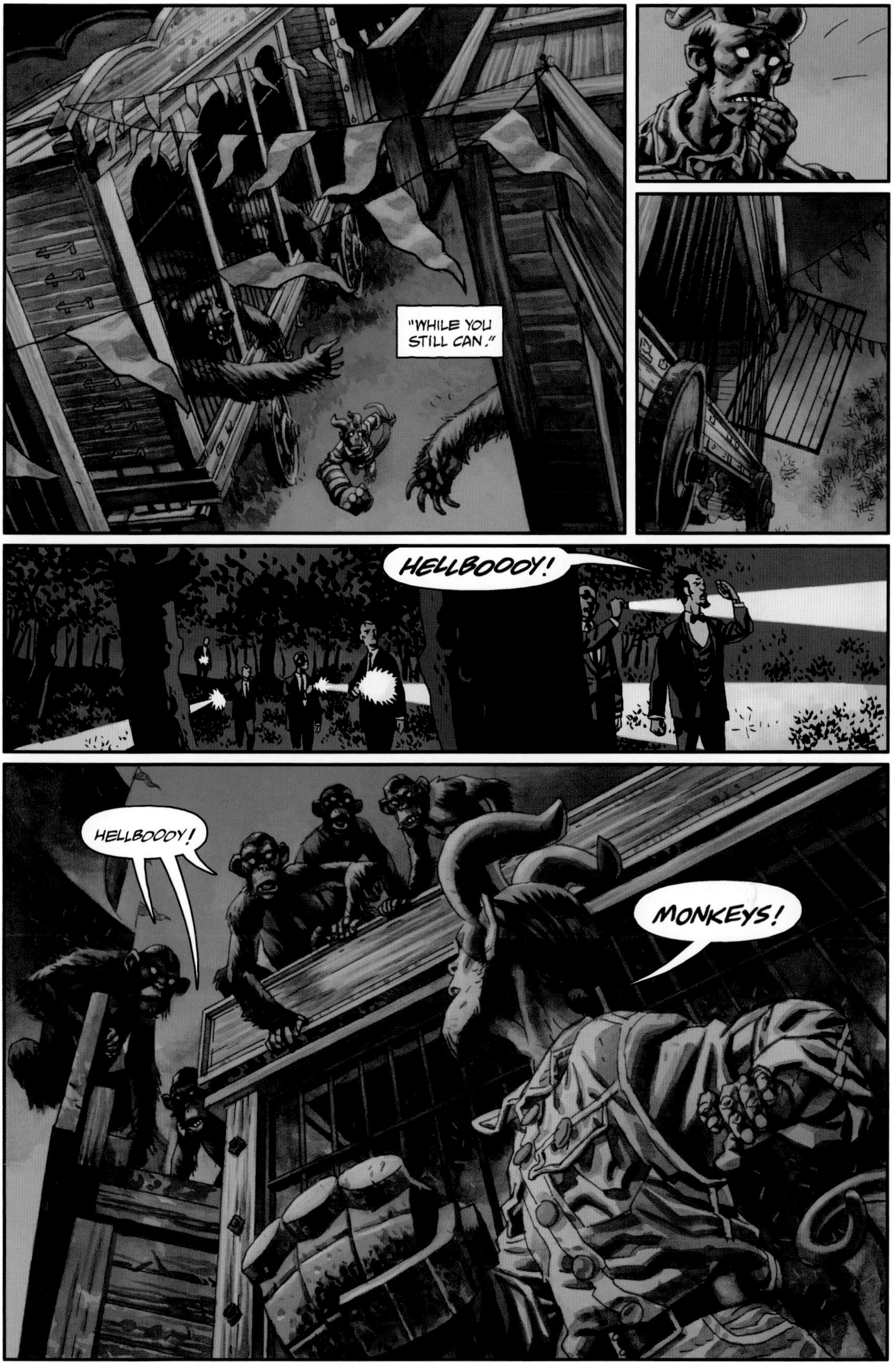
"WHILE YOU STILL CAN."
HELLBOOOY!
HELLBOOOY!
MONKEYS!

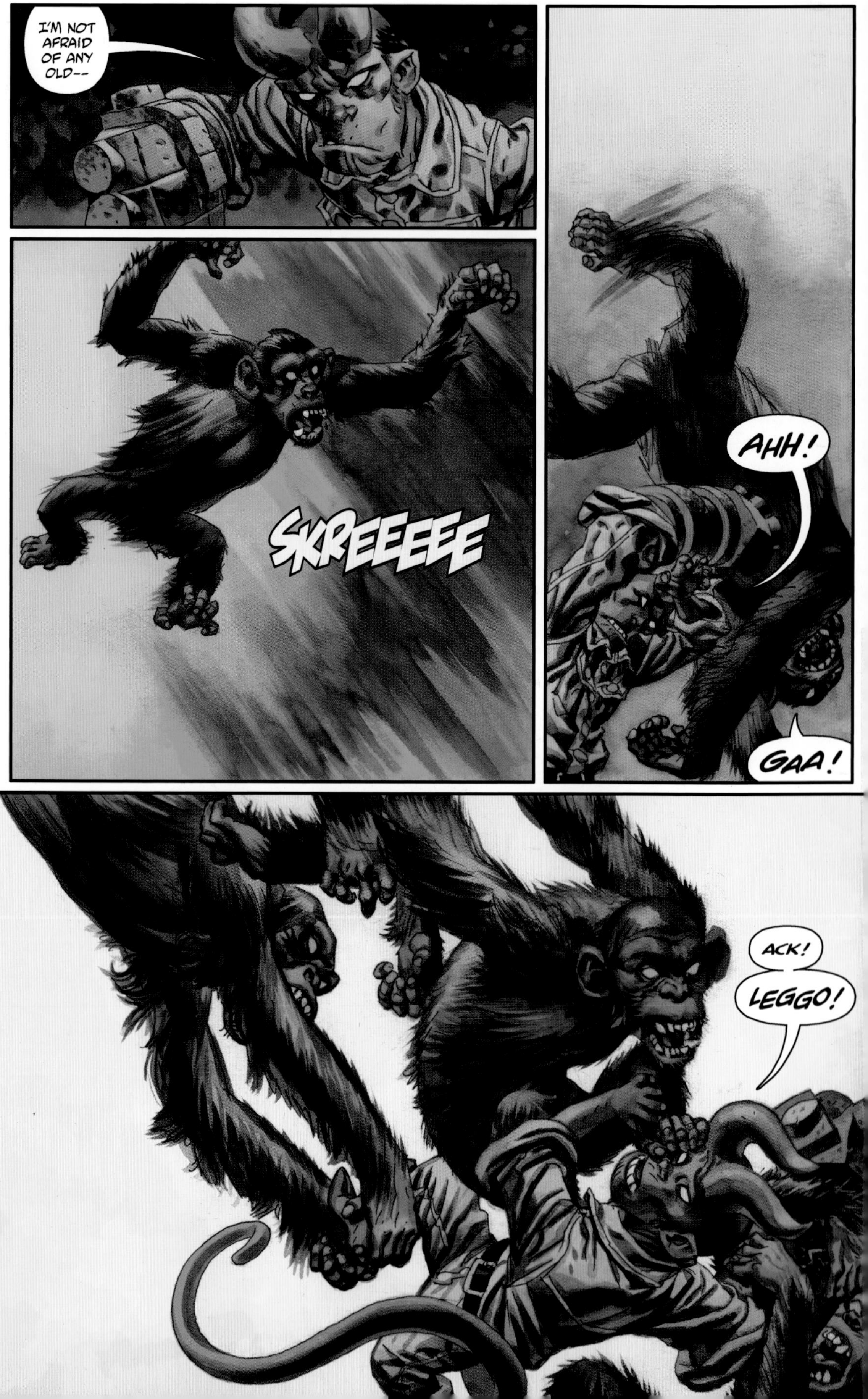

I'M NOT AFRAID OF ANY OLD--
SKREEEEEE
AHH!
GAA!
ACK!
LEGGO!

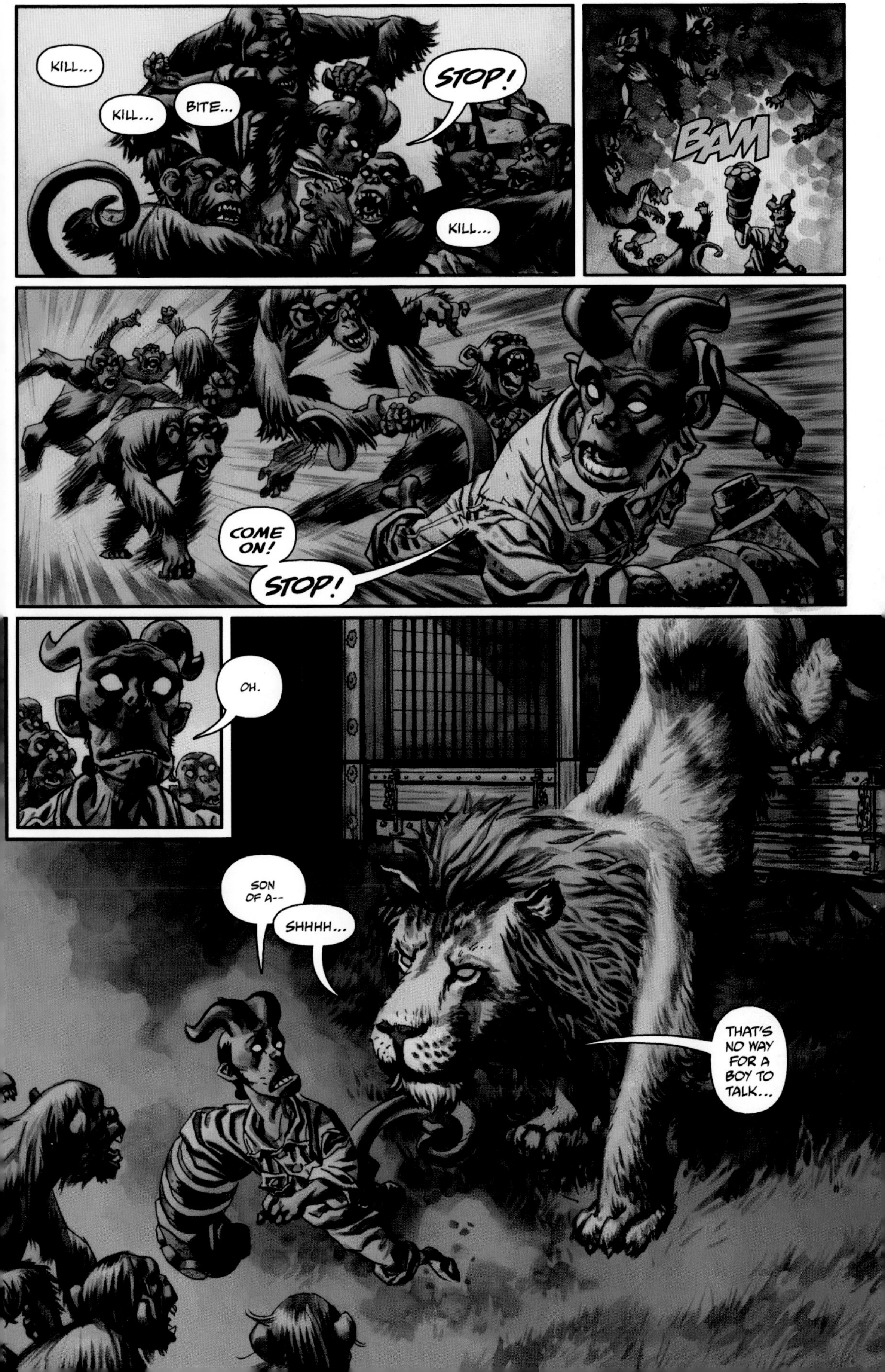
KILL...
KILL...
BITE...
STOP!
KILL...
BAM
COME ON!
STOP!
OH.
SON OF A--
SHHHH...
THAT'S NO WAY FOR A BOY TO TALK...

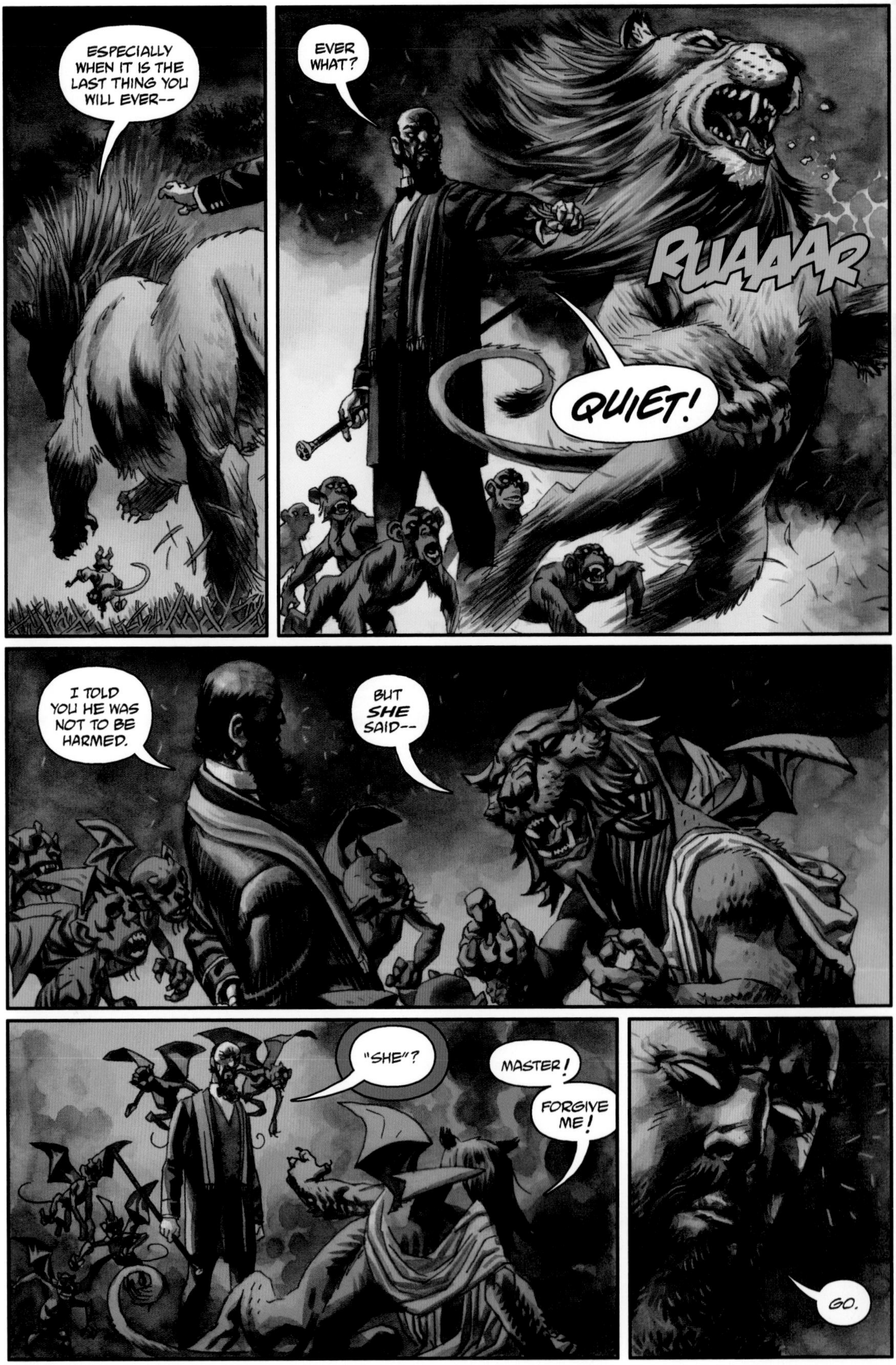
ESPECIALLY WHEN IT IS THE LAST THING YOU WILL EVER--
EVER WHAT?
RUAAAR
QUIET!
I TOLD YOU HE WAS NOT TO BE HARMED.
BUT SHE SAID--
"SHE"?
MASTER!
FORGIVE ME!
GO.

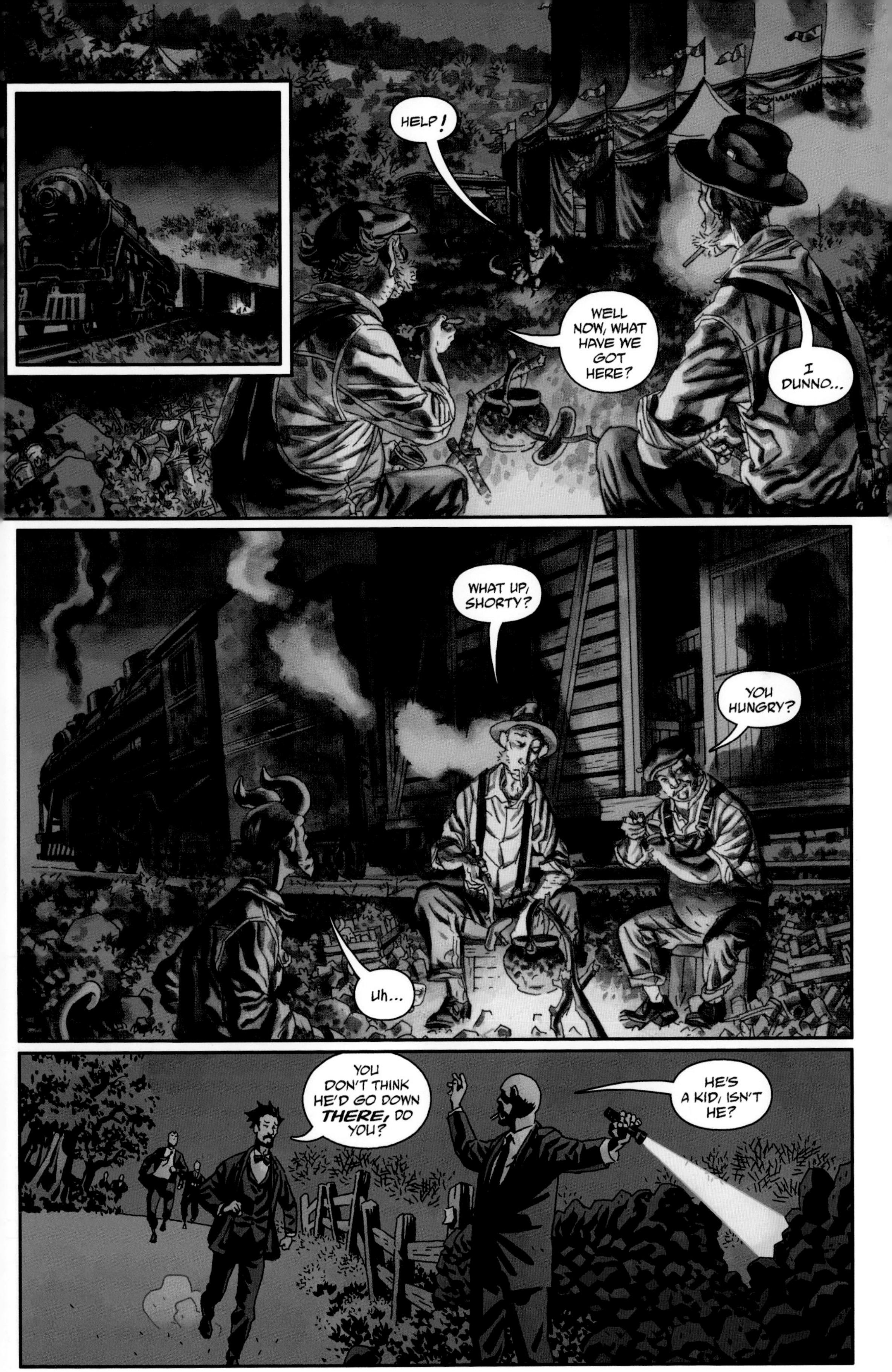
HELP!
WELL NOW, WHAT HAVE WE GOT HERE?
I DUNNO...
WHAT UP, SHORTY?
YOU HUNGRY?
Uh...
YOU DON'T THINK HE'D GO DOWN **THERE,** DO YOU?
HE'S A KID, ISN'T HE?

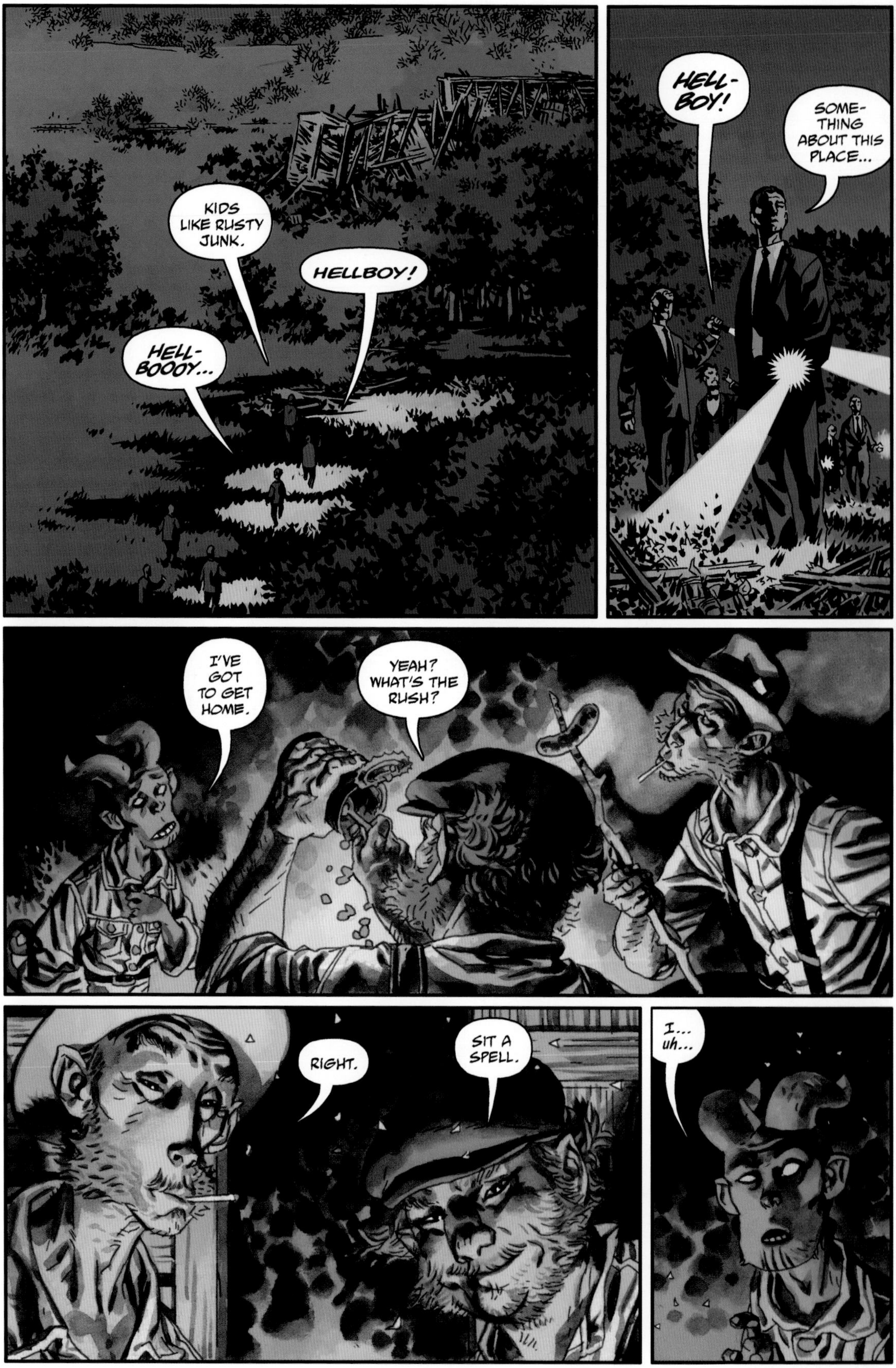
KIDS LIKE RUSTY JUNK.
HELLBOY!
HELL-BOOOY...
HELL-BOY!
SOME-THING ABOUT THIS PLACE...
I'VE GOT TO GET HOME.
YEAH? WHAT'S THE RUSH?
RIGHT.
SIT A SPELL.
I... uh...

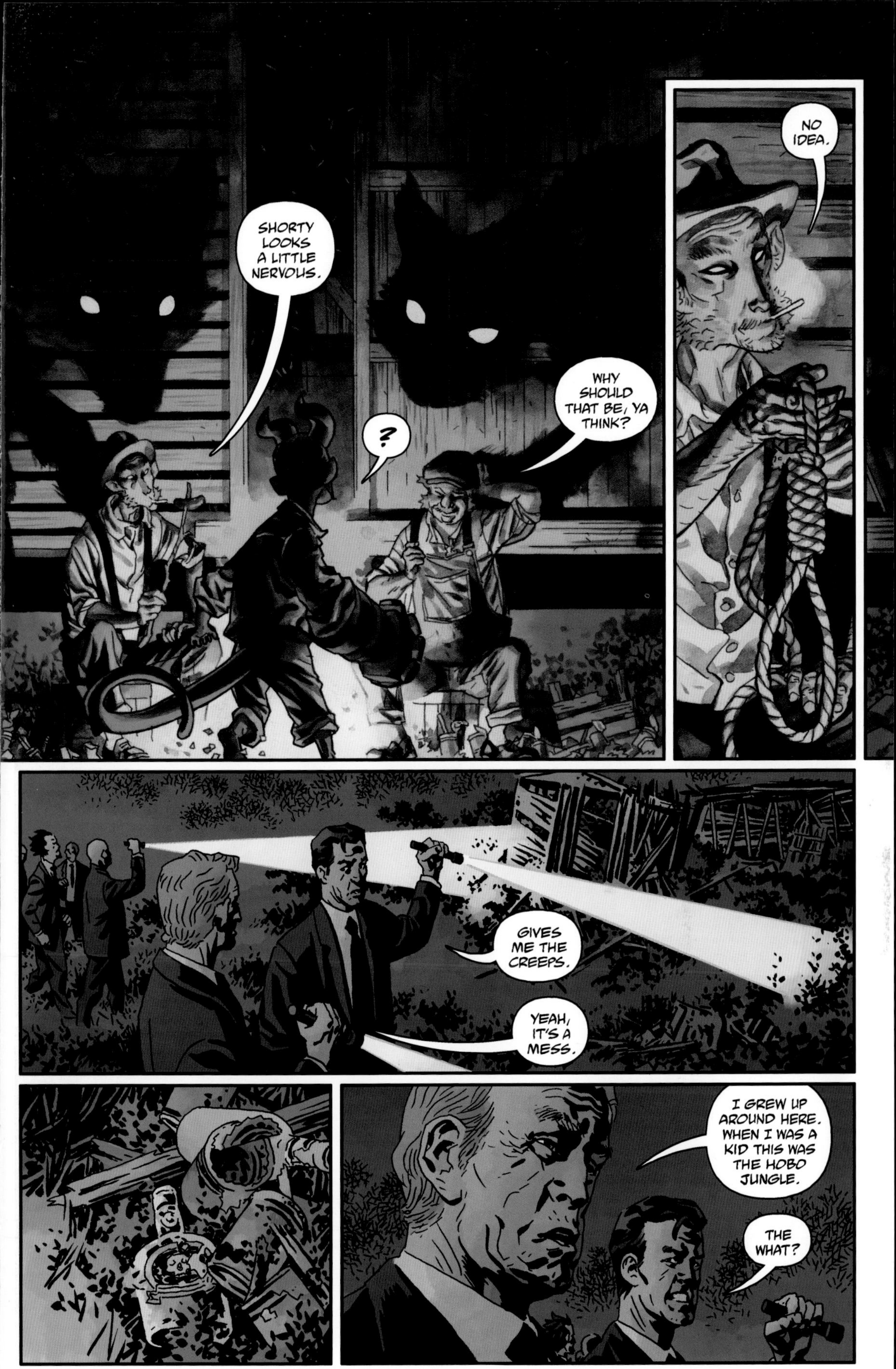
SHORTY LOOKS A LITTLE NERVOUS.
?
WHY SHOULD THAT BE, YA THINK?
NO IDEA.
GIVES ME THE CREEPS.
YEAH, IT'S A MESS.
I GREW UP AROUND HERE. WHEN I WAS A KID THIS WAS THE HOBO JUNGLE.
THE WHAT?

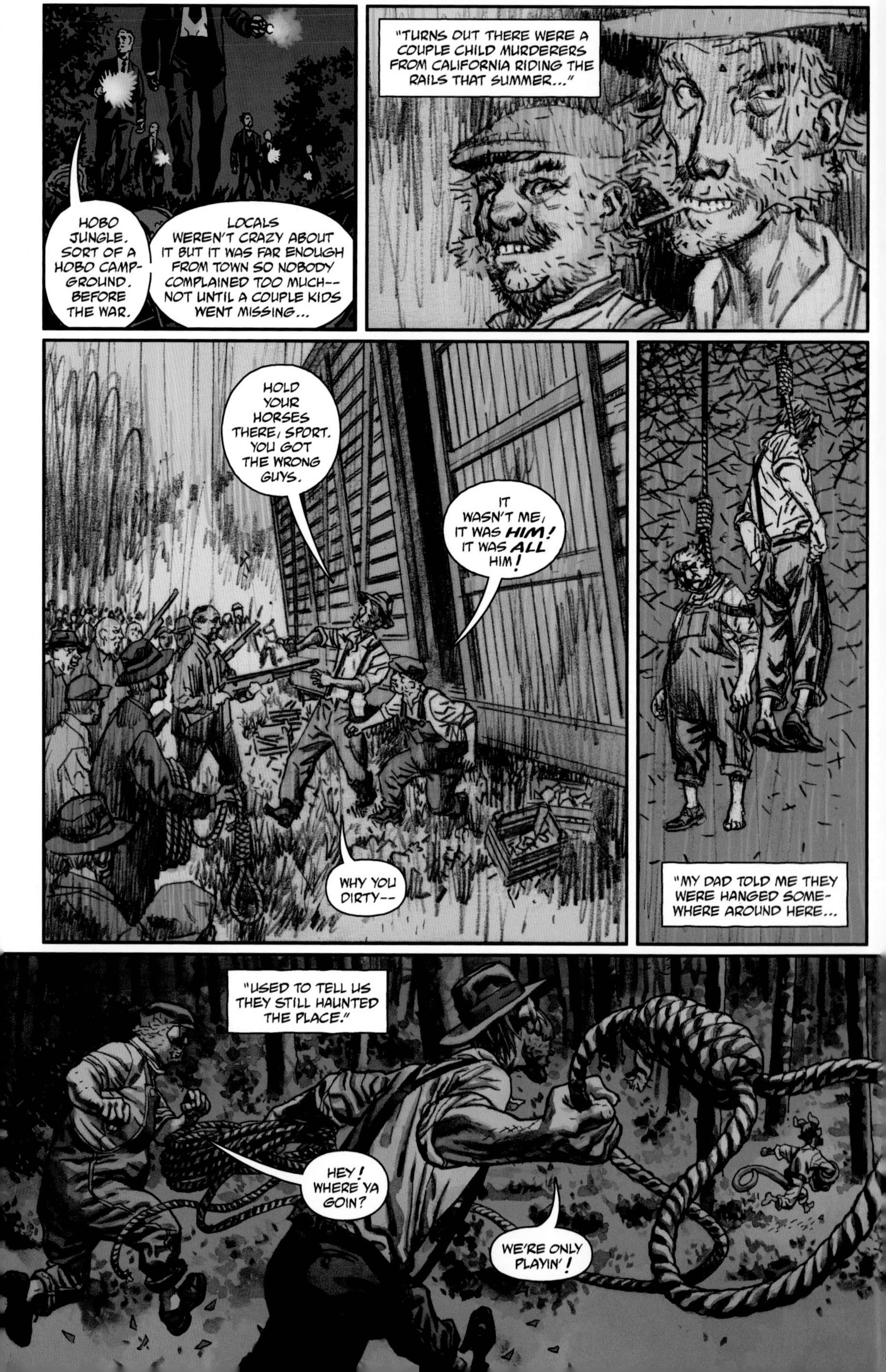
HOBO JUNGLE. SORT OF A HOBO CAMPGROUND. BEFORE THE WAR.
LOCALS WEREN'T CRAZY ABOUT IT BUT IT WAS FAR ENOUGH FROM TOWN SO NOBODY COMPLAINED TOO MUCH-- NOT UNTIL A COUPLE KIDS WENT MISSING...
"TURNS OUT THERE WERE A COUPLE CHILD MURDERERS FROM CALIFORNIA RIDING THE RAILS THAT SUMMER..."
HOLD YOUR HORSES THERE, SPORT. YOU GOT THE WRONG GUYS.
IT WASN'T ME, IT WAS HIM! IT WAS ALL HIM!
WHY YOU DIRTY--
"MY DAD TOLD ME THEY WERE HANGED SOMEWHERE AROUND HERE...
"USED TO TELL US THEY STILL HAUNTED THE PLACE."
HEY! WHERE YA GOIN?
WE'RE ONLY PLAYIN'!

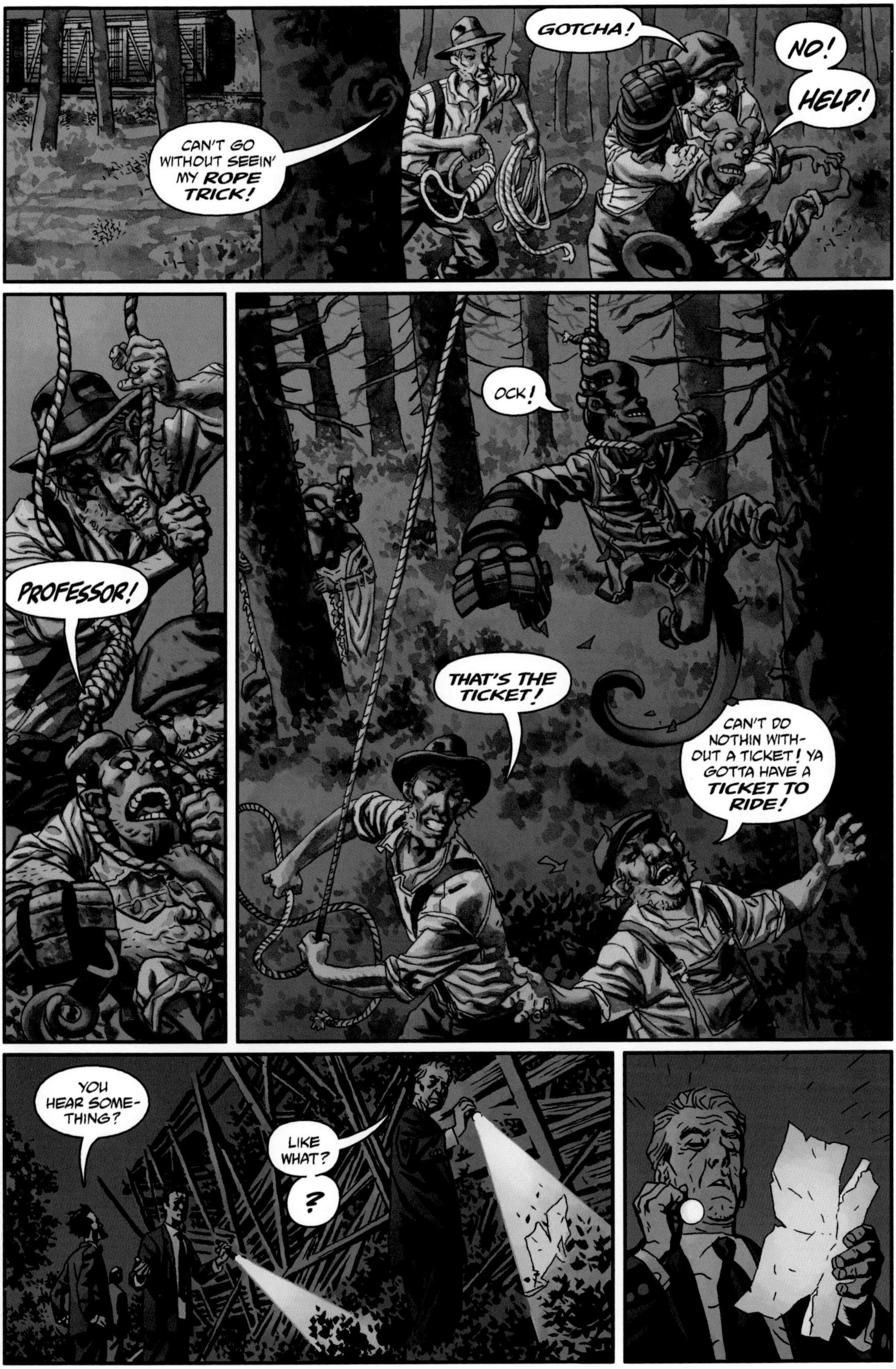
CAN'T GO WITHOUT SEEIN' MY ROPE TRICK!
GOTCHA!
NO!
HELP!
PROFESSOR!
OCK!
THAT'S THE TICKET!
CAN'T DO NOTHIN WITH-OUT A TICKET! YA GOTTA HAVE A TICKET TO RIDE!
YOU HEAR SOME-THING?
LIKE WHAT?
?

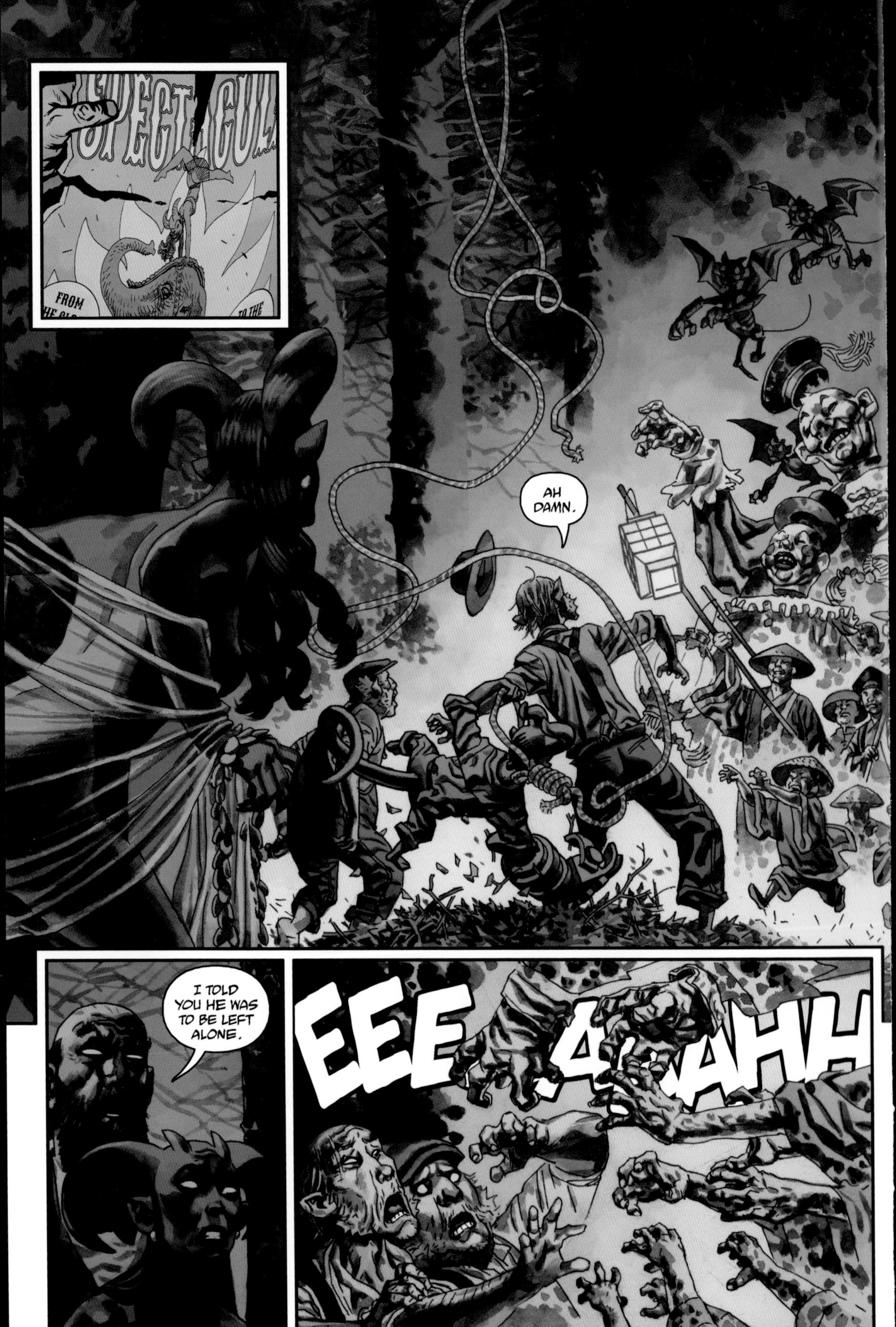

SPECTACUL
FROM
TO THE
AH DAMN.
I TOLD YOU HE WAS TO BE LEFT ALONE.
EEE
AHH

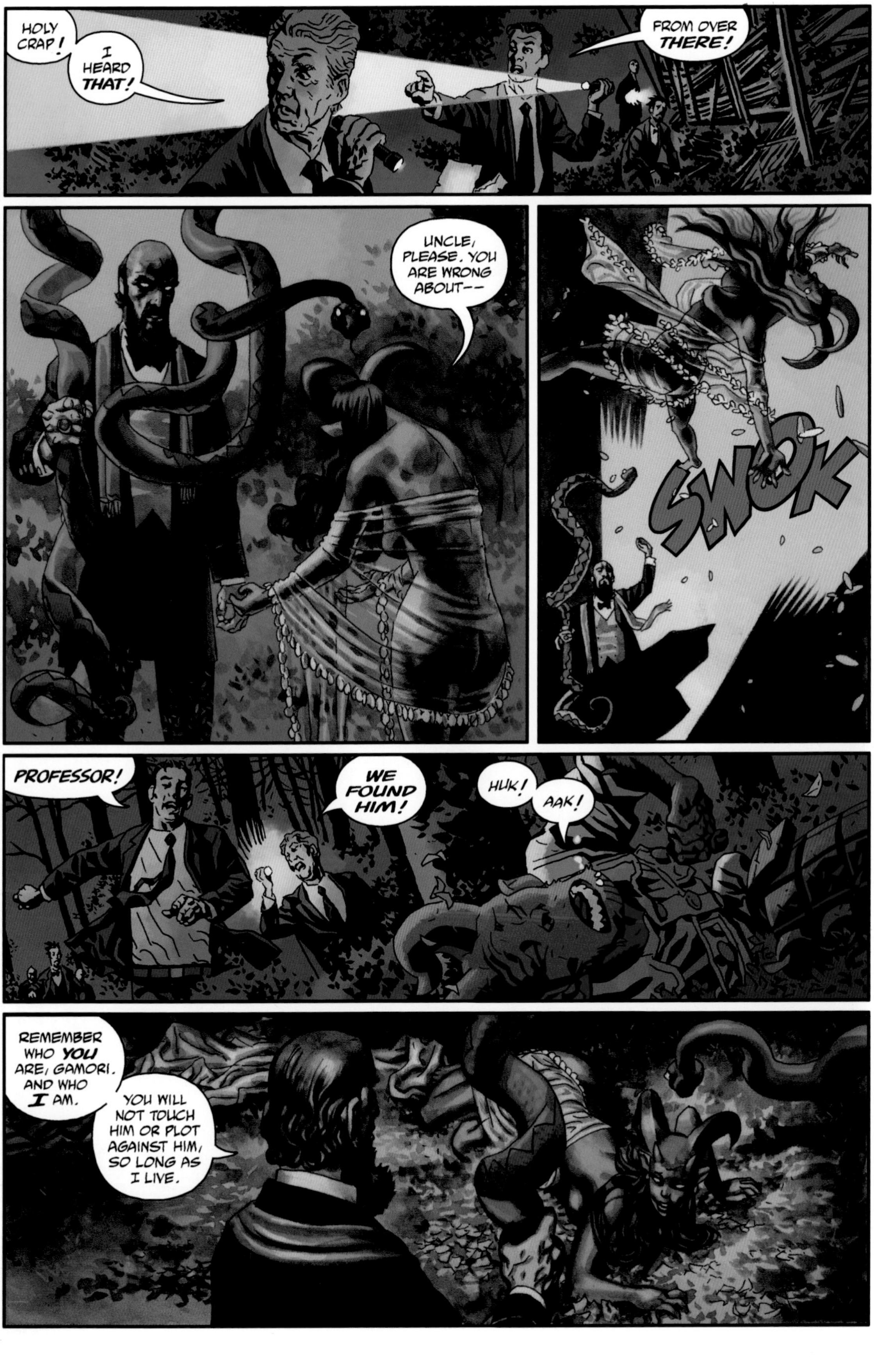
HOLY CRAP!
I HEARD THAT!
FROM OVER THERE!
UNCLE, PLEASE. YOU ARE WRONG ABOUT--
SWOK
PROFESSOR!
WE FOUND HIM!
HUK!
AAK!
REMEMBER WHO YOU ARE, GAMORI. AND WHO I AM.
YOU WILL NOT TOUCH HIM OR PLOT AGAINST HIM, SO LONG AS I LIVE.

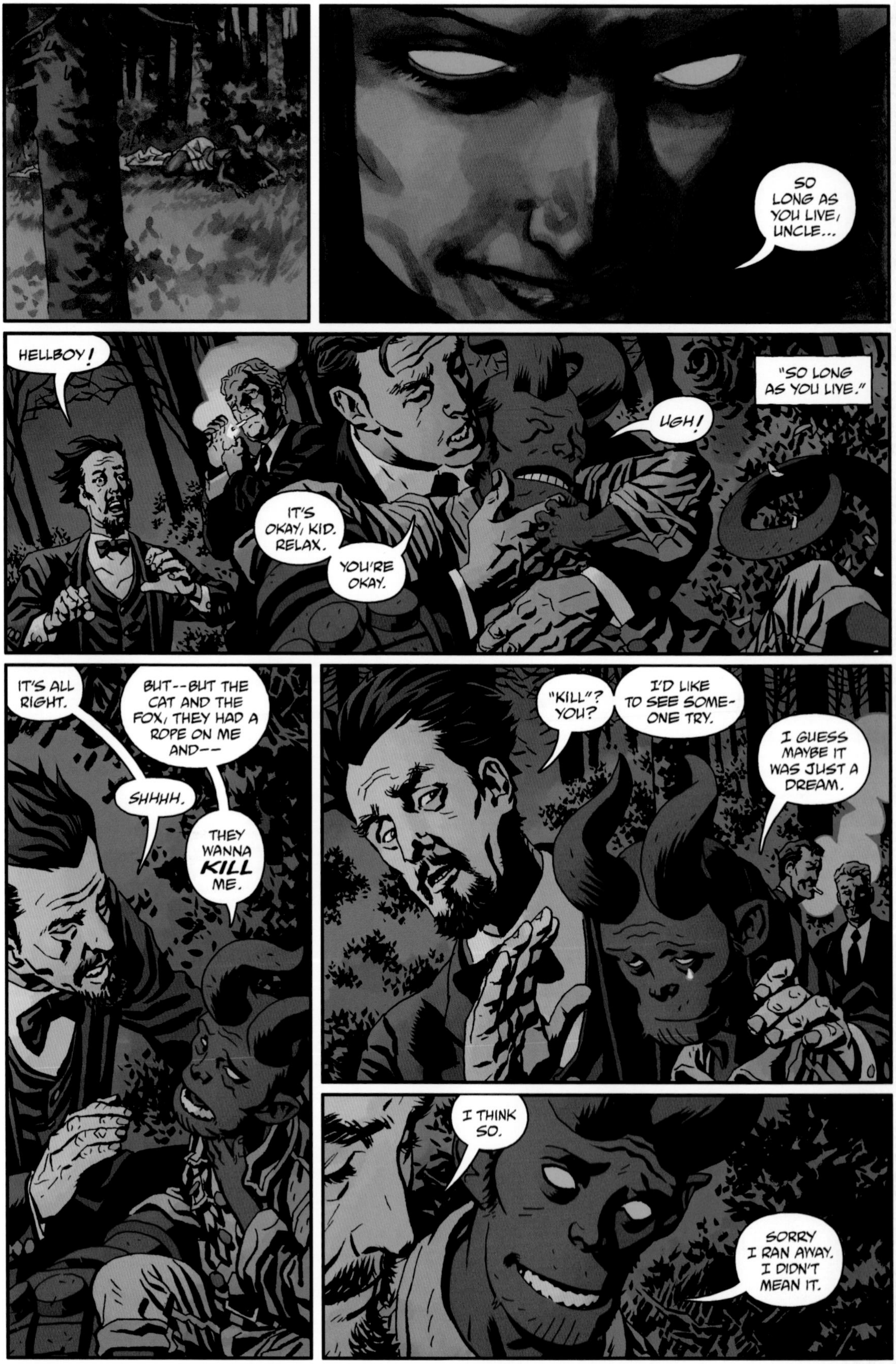
SO LONG AS YOU LIVE, UNCLE...
HELLBOY!
"SO LONG AS YOU LIVE."
UGH!
IT'S OKAY, KID. RELAX.
YOU'RE OKAY.
IT'S ALL RIGHT.
BUT--BUT THE CAT AND THE FOX, THEY HAD A ROPE ON ME AND--
SHHHH.
THEY WANNA KILL ME.
"KILL"? YOU?
I'D LIKE TO SEE SOME-ONE TRY.
I GUESS MAYBE IT WAS JUST A DREAM.
I THINK SO.
SORRY I RAN AWAY. I DIDN'T MEAN IT.

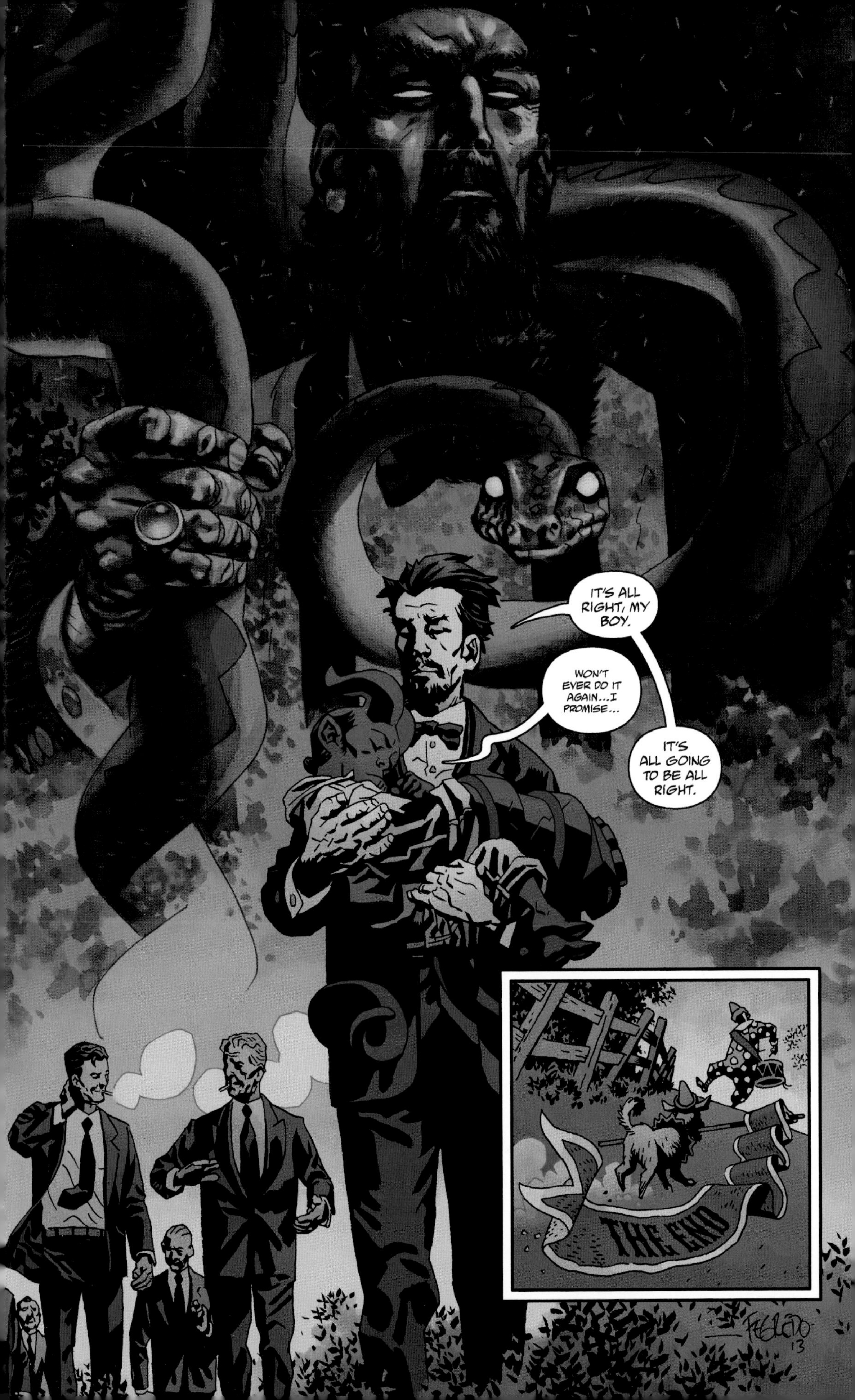
IT'S ALL RIGHT, MY BOY.
WON'T EVER DO IT AGAIN...I PROMISE...
IT'S ALL GOING TO BE ALL RIGHT.
THE END